D1269899

The Betting Man

This second edition consists of:

1,195 copies for sale
of which this is number   2 7 3

and 95 copies for the author's use
of which this is number   ___

The Betting Man

A Racing Biography of William Hill

The King of the Bookies

by
Joe Ward Hill

ELCOTT

ELCOTT BOOKS
The Lamb Yard, The Parade, Marlborough, Wilts, SN8 1BR

c/o Professional Book Sales
4 Arran Quay, Dublin 7

c/o Mitty's of Queen Street,
9 Queen Street, Melbourne 3000, Victoria, Australia

First edition in January, 1993
Second edition in March, 1993
© Joe Ward Hill

ISBN 1–874561–00–1

Printed by The Cromwell Press,
Broughton Gifford, Melksham, Wiltshire SN12 8PH

Contents

Foreword

William Hill was unquestionably the greatest individual book-maker to stand in the ring this century.

In 1929, as a young man of twenty-six, he arrived in London from Birmingham full of ruthless ambition and drive. For the next eleven or twelve years he made a book at Northolt Park Pony Races, at the Dogs and at the Holiday Meetings such as Epsom, Goodwood and Ascot.

In 1941 he bet on the rails for the first time and by 1945 was King of the Ring. From then he bet in the proverbial 'telephone' numbers until the Royal Ascot meeting of 1955 when he decided that the money had dried up – it had in his terms – and he never bet on the racecourse again.

I knew William Hill well from March 1933 until his death in October 1971. In the early days at Northolt we had one or two brushes when he thought that the SP was too much in the punters favour, although the most serious row was in 1939. He 'knocked out' a pony of his, Win Over, from 5-2 to 100-30 and as he was the only bookmaker going that price we returned at 5-2. We made it up the day War broke out and never had a cross word for over thirty years.

William, as well as being a mathematical genius, was an authority on breeding. He bred Nimbus the 1949 Derby winner and the 1959 St. Leger winner Cantelo.

I am delighted that Joe Ward Hill, his youngest brother, has written such an authoritative account of his life.

William was a legend in his own life time and remains so today.

Geoffrey Hamlyn
December 1992.

Current day monetary values have been inserted in certain places in brackets – see pages 125/126 for a full footnote.

1

Inevitably, when a man rises as high and fast in his profession as my brother William, he has his detractors. While it is not my intention to portray William as a candidate for canonisation, I hope to convince readers that most of the accusations levelled at him were the result of jealousy. To succeed as a bookmaker a man must be tough both mentally and physically, and the qualities that brought William to the top, and then kept him there, were his enterprise and ruthless energy, allied to his tireless search for business, both on the racecourse and in the office. Charm is a quality of which bookmakers usually had in short supply, but my brother possessed it in abundance, when he chose to exercise it. No matter how busy he was, every customer received a smile and with his retentive memory he never forgot a name. More than six feet tall and broad shouldered, he was handsome in a rugged sort of way. He was always immaculately turned out, usually in a double-breasted dark suit, white collar and black bowler or Homburg hat and did not conform with most punters' idea of a bookmaker. He was almost certainly the only one to possess 'panache'. Furthermore, the sign above his betting board (before he moved on to the rails) 'Courtesy, civility and integrity', meant what it said.

Geoffrey Hamlyn who knew William Hill from the time he started betting at the pony racing meeting at Northolt in 1933, remembers that William created a sensation by opening his book there an hour before the first race and announcing in stentorian tones: "Starting price anywhere, SP."

It was at Northolt Park that William blossomed into a national bookmaker and from total obscurity his name became a household word within ten years. Geoffrey went on to tell me that in well over forty years, during which time he returned the starting prices for *The Sporting Life*, he has never seen a bookmaker to touch him. He could do twice the business in half the time of any other bookmaker. The bookmakers who ruled the roost prior to the arrival of William, with the notable exceptions of Harry 'Snouty' Parker and Billy Chandler, the late uncle of Victor, were an unenterprising lot, and William revealed his contempt for their orthodox methods by his readiness to take a gamble when

9

he thought it was warranted. This flamboyance in their eyes was courting disaster and they comforted themselves with the thought that this 'upstart' could not last long. They were wrong and this increased their dislike of him.

By and large, sixty years ago, bookmakers were uneducated and, except for mastering a set of figures, (known to the trade as 'reckoning up odds'), were content to remain so. William's education was sketchy to say the least of it but throughout his career, he was forever searching for knowledge which might help him succeed in his profession. If ever a man could be termed single-minded, it was my brother, and no amount of adversity (of which there was plenty), could deviate from his purpose of becoming the most successful racecourse bookmaker in the history of the Turf.

When William first came to London from Birmingham in 1929, bookmakers were far from popular, as gang warfare between the two cities had only recently been stamped out by the courage of a body of men, chiefly ex-service men and policemen, organised by the late Major Wymer, known as Jockey Club Personnel, and the forerunner of the present Racecourse Security Services.

The subsequent improvement of the bookmakers' image was mainly due to two men, William Hill and Archie Scott. Though the latter was hardly known to the public, he rendered immeasurable services to the profession behind the scenes.

By a quirk of fate, these two men came to work under one roof. The firm of A. C. Scott Ltd. was bought by Alfred Cope in 1957 and in turn was taken over by William Hill in 1962. Scott became a director of the Hill Organisation, and shared the executive suite in Hill House with William and his accountant, Lionel Barber, who later became the first chairman of Holders Investment Trust, under which name the William Hill firm became the first bookmakers' business to be quoted on the Stock Exchange. Broadly speaking this concern was the work of three men of outstanding ability, William Hill, Lionel Barber and Bill Balshaw. William was the complete bookmaker, with every fact of his trade at his fingertips. Barber was the accountant, with a financial capacity amounting to near genius. Balshaw's accomplishments were less spectacular, but he ran Hill's Glasgow office for twenty years and was chairman of the company from 1967 to 1972. It was he and Jack Swift who finally succeeded in pushing William, albeit reluctantly, into betting shops, upon which of course the big bookmaking firms depend nowadays for the majority of their profits.

2

William, number three in a family of thirteen, was born in Birmingham on July 16, 1903. He was a delicate child and was in and out of hospital most of the time. He therefore did not go to school until he was eight years old and he then attended Small Heath School in Birmingham. He was so backward that he could not keep pace with his contemporaries and was put at the back of the class, drawing and painting for which he showed considerable aptitude indeed, at a school exhibition he had a section to himself. A fond aunt described him as a 'boy wonder' after he had 'flogged' one of his drawings for a pound. William had no illusions that he could make a commercial success of painting a pretty picture. Art for art's sake and a life of penury was not his idea of a profession.

A conviction which remained with him all his life was that money might not be everything, but it was an essential adjunct to happiness. He always regarded poverty as the number one enemy of mankind. One occasion on which William employed his artistic ability was when he designed a poster for his first fixed odds football coupon, which netted him only six pounds! Later, this form of wagering earned the organisation many millions of pounds.

It may be worth noting that our father was not only a painter of coaches in the early years of the century, but was responsible for the complicated heraldic designs and crests with which all horsedrawn coaches were then adorned. One of father's sisters also became a successful artist.

Father died in middle age, but our mother lived to a ripe old age. She and William were devoted to one another, and he saw to it that she lacked for nothing. She often told all her friends how lucky she was to have such a dutiful son. Being twenty years younger than William, I did not see a great deal of him for a number of years, but in later life we became very close and I became as keen as he on the breeding of horses. Under the name of Ward Hill, I built up a thriving bookmaking business with headquarters at Stevenage and also founded a stud there, which has bred a number of winners.

In William's early years, 'flogging' was a way of life, and every object was appraised on how much it would fetch. He had a persuasive tongue and at an early age could strike a hard bargain. This technique was to serve him well in years to come. William would have been a match for any stallholder in an oriental bazaar.

At the age of twelve our family left Birmingham, and during the First World War, father was posted to the BSA works, and we went to live in Barnacle, near Coventry. William had to walk several miles to school in the next village but only stood it for a week before he walked out. As far as I know, this was the end of his formal education. Everything he learned subsequently was self taught.

William's first job was on a farm, where his employer combined the jobs of butcher and publican. The *red-letter* day of William's week was Tuesday, when he attended Nuneaton market. Apart from the excitement of the market atmosphere, he was allowed to drive the newly purchased cattle back home. William's other job was to drive his boss's horse and trap around the adjacent villages collecting orders for meat. He found this life very agreeable and it gave him a lasting love of the countryside. Unfortunately, eighteen months later, father was moved by BSA back to Birmingham, and he took William with him. Back there, father started his own workshop as a coach painter but, as he was required for war work, William ran the coach painting business with four or five older men under him. For a blissful month or two, the fifteen year old William was earning about £25 a week, a fabulous sum in 1918. Father took the view, however, that this was not good for William, so he apprenticed him to a tool making subsidiary of BSA at a salary of 7s 6d a week of which he gave mother 5s.

Back to square one, William again had to live by his wits, and his first venture was to run a weekly dance in the village of Acocks Green, for which he designed and painted all the posters. He became a proficient ballroom dancer, and gave exhibition dances with his girl-friend, which earned him a couple of extra guineas every Saturday. He also sold ice creams during the intervals.

At the age of eighteen, in February, 1921, an entirely new chapter in William's life began. He joined the Royal Irish Constabulary, and was posted to Mallow, Co. Cork, and did his early training at Gormanstown.

All sorts of reasons have been put forward as to why William took this step, but it can be answered in one word – money. £500 [£16,000] on enlistment, plus a further £500 on retirement. He knew little or nothing about the Irish 'troubles', although later, he developed strong, left-wing, political views. The R.I.C. had a high record of service and discipline, and is not to be confused with the Auxiliary Force, recruited by Lloyd George and, later known as the 'Black and Tans.' This outfit was responsible for many grave excesses. In 1922 the R.I.C. was disbanded and its counterpart in the north became the Royal Ulster Constabulary.

With his £500 [£16,000] gratuity, William began to make a book, touring the Midland pubs on an elderly motor cycle. The going was slow, so with the help of an old bookmaker who acted as his clerk, he attended Uttoxeter races, with disastrous results.

With what remained of his £500, he rented an SP office in Pershore Street, Birmingham, and at the age of twenty, got married. Ivy his wife, was a ladies' hairdresser, and they at once opened a business together.

Although William hardly conformed to most people's idea of a perfect husband, everyone who knew them agreed that Ivy was always the perfect wife. Blonde and beautiful, she combined charm with a shrewd appraisal of the character of others. They were married for forty-eight years, and the one great sorrow of both their lives was the tragic death of their daughter, Kathleen Lavinia St. George, at the age of thirty-seven.

In his will, William stated: "I wish to place on record my sincere appreciation of the love, loyalty and devotion of my wife throughout our married life."

The hairdressing business thrived to such an extent that he closed the SP business. But William was far too ambitious to spend the remainder of his days in the reflected glory of a successful wife, and after a few months he began to bet in the cheap rings at what he termed the 'carnival' meetings, Epsom, Ascot, Goodwood and Doncaster. More often than not, he returned from these meetings, having 'done in' some of the profits from Ivy's business, but he was learning the bookmakers' trade the hard way.

3

In 1929 William went to London and the next ten years were decisive for him. He was betting on the dogs in the cheap rings at Harringay and the White City, where his business acumen quickly out-classed that of the opposition, and where he was soon giving out between 1,000 and 1,200 betting tickets every night, which represents a lot of business. He also started betting at Northolt Park and Portsmouth Park at the new and thriving sport of pony racing.

In addition, William made an illegal book in the Pelican Club in Denman Street, London W.1. Here he used what was to become the betting shop technique of a blackboard showing the runners and riders, with the results chalked up from a tape machine. He did not rely on the modern methods of 'shows' to make a book. These 'shows' represent the price at which either the horses or the dogs are quoted on the track. William betted to his own figures, based on his now extensive knowledge of form and 'values.' The club enjoyed tremendous popularity in the West End and was packed for a year before it was raided and closed down. William was fined. While it lasted, this business was not only profitable but also provided William with invaluable experience and increased his self confidence. By the time the Magistrates closed him down, he had all the tricks of the book-making trade at his fingertips.

Strong-arm methods were the order of the day in many of the cheaper rings, and particularly on the outside pitches, when William started his career as a racecourse bookmaker. It was no rarity for a punter to be told when he went to draw his winnings that he had backed something else. The bookmaker would accompany this information with a gesture of his thumb over his shoulder in the direction of a formidable looking bruiser, and the advice to push off – or else!

William profited from the behaviour of these strong-arm 'welshers' as it soon became appreciated that his methods were in direct contrast to those of his rivals, while his immaculate appearance contrasted with the cloth cap and check suits all around him. Not only were William's clients certain that they would be paid their winnings, but that they would be paid with a smile, something which had never happened before. On one occasion, a punter who had enjoyed a nice 'touch' expressed the view that that young man would go far. "Yes," replied his friend, "and not like these other beggars, with their punters in hot pursuit, hollering for their dough."

William betted for a few weeks on the boards at Northolt under the name of Albert (Buck) Carr, but after a short while he moved to the rails, and for the first time found himself in competition with some of the big names of the bookmaking fraternity. Undaunted, he soon became one of the leaders of the ring, and by the time Northolt closed down, with the outbreak of World War II, William was doing far more business than any other bookmaker, at a meeting which provided a stronger market than that at a number of meetings under Jockey Club Rules. William's interest in Northolt was not confined to making a book, and it was there that he became an owner for the first time. After a somewhat inauspicious start, he owned a very good colt called Win Over, who dead-heated for second place in the Northolt Derby of 1939. The winner was the Hon. Dorothy Paget's Scottish Rifle, a son of the Epsom Derby winner, Cameronian.

William met Miss Paget for the first time after this race for the Northolt Derby, and though she subsequently became a valued client of the firm, that was the extent of their relationship.

Soon after the war, there were rumours in racing circles, that William reached the top of the tree in such a short time, because he and Miss Paget were very close and that she had financed him and made his success possible. This, had it been true, would have been the only time in the history of gambling that a backer had subsidised a layer so that he or she could win or lose from him.

Miss Paget, 'Queen Of The Turf', hated men, and the more masculine they were the more they repelled her. It is, therefore, obvious that although she liked doing business with William, when they were separated by the 'rails', he would venture any closer to her at his peril. With the outbreak of war, William's first venture as a London racecourse bookmaker came to an end. He had never betted in the south on the rails, and had often said that his ambition was confined to making about £100,000, [around £3,000,000] enough to buy a farm with sufficient gallops to train ponies to run at Northolt. He had no desire at that stage of his life to become a national bookmaker.

18

When William left Birmingham for London in 1929, he burned his boats. But his business acumen and good manners quickly earned him a host of new clients in the metropolitan area. In 1934, he opened a small office in Jermyn Street, over Barnards the Hatters. The staff consisted of William and three clerks. There, and on the racecourse, business prospered, largely on account of his energy and refusal to relax and be satisfied.

So successful was his search for new clients that it soon became apparent that the minute premises in Jermyn Street could no longer cope with the growing business.

William, therefore, looked for a larger office, in the same vicinity. He found what he wanted in Park Lane, the former residence of Lord Inchcape, backing on to Curzon Street. He could have hardly chosen a worse time to expand. War with Germany was now inevitable. It was apparent that Hitler would march into Poland when he considered the moment propitious, in which case Chamberlain would have no alternative than to forsake his policy of appeasement.

By now William was a national bookmaker and once the decision to leave Jermyn Street had been taken, he had to compete with the long established firms with inexhaustible resources or perish. For probably the only time in his life, William was downcast, and told Geoffrey Hamlyn that he would not be able to keep up with the heavy rental on his new Park Lane premises, adding: "I see nothing for it but to disband my organisation, and think of something else." Far from disbanding, the very opposite proved to be the case and, had he but known it, the vast Hill organisation was about to come into being.

William was not called up for military service, owing to his poor record of health during his youth he was therefore put into the lowest medical category. He went ahead with his plans as though the war did not exist and by 1942, after some nerve-racking experiences, when it must have been touch and go as to whether he could carry on, he was the acknowledged leader of the ring and was collecting clients and goodwill on a scale which even he had never thought possible.

It is deplorable, but nevertheless true, that many racing people, including the bookmakers, regarded the war as a tedious interruption of their normal activities. As an industry, racing has always been self-centred, which, in peace time, may be no bad

19

thing. But it is quite another matter when the country is fighting for its existence.

If a bomb fell on Clapham Junction, most racegoers would have been more concerned as to whether the trains to Windsor or Salisbury – the only two south country racecourses functioning apart from Newmarket – would be delayed, rather than displaying any concern as to how many casualties had been inflicted. It was a wise policy on the part of the Government to permit a modicum of racing as an essential aid in maintaining the breeding industry. But, sad to relate, there was considerable abuse of this concession. On St. Leger day at Newmarket in September, 1942, when there was no basic petrol allowance, the car parks were crammed to overflowing with vehicles of all kinds and attendance was a record for the July course.

The first of the William Hill companies was formed in May, 1939. William Hill Ltd. was registered as a private company with a nominal capital of £10,000 in shares of £1 each. An agreement between the company and William Hill, provided for the allotment to him of £5,000 five per cent preference shares, and a salary of £1,250 a year, plus £1,000 for personal expenses. Mr. Sam Seeman, a London cinema owner, had a twenty per cent interest in the business. He was a great help to William in the world of commerce and advertising, of which at that time William knew very little. Seeman convinced him of the power of advertising, and once the lesson was learned, it was never forgotten.

4

Just before the outbreak of war, William had begun to advertise in a big way. Starting in the *Greyhound Express*, he went on to buy considerable space in *The Sporting Life*. At this time, the six most prolific advertising bookmakers were J. John, James Maclean, David Cope, Joe Lee, Douglas Stuart and Scotland & Co. In September, 1939, the situation was ominous and these six firms held a meeting under the chairmanship of Alfred Cope and agreed to cut down their advertising to the minimum. William, however, had put everything he had into establishing his business and he had to go on advertising in order to survive. Although the business was being run on a shoestring, he took every bit of advertising space available, and by the end of the war was probably the leading advertising bookmaker, in addition to being firmly established on the racecourse.

William's decision to continue advertising when owing to the shortage of racing there was little business to advertise, brought down the wrath of the six above mentioned firms on his head. It was one of the few occasions when bookmakers have cooperated with one another. Usually, they are too busy bickering among themselves to form a united front. When war broke out, the Doncaster St. Leger meeting was cancelled and no racing took place for several weeks. Although his business was completely solvent, William was desperately short of ready cash to meet his commitments – the most pressing being the heavy rental of his Park Lane office. Things picked up a little during the spring of 1940, and he was in the position to open an ante-post book on the Derby.

It was at this meeting that William betted on the rails on the July course at Newmarket for the first time. The firm occupies more or less the same pitch today. The leading bookmakers had always betted at the top end of the rails, but William, with tongue in his cheek, took up his position among the smaller fry, where up until that time few bets of more than a pound or two had been struck. In next to no time, the 'market' had moved down to Hill's pitch, and he was soon taking more money than the aristocrats in at what had always been regarded as the most favourable of pitches. Business was almost back to normal by

1941 and William described the market at Manchester, where the St. Leger was run, and won by Sun Castle at 10–1, as particularly strong.

Although there were many reverses to come, particularly in the Far East, a spirit of optimism prevailed towards the end of 1942, and the interest in war time racing was enormous. That year King George VI owned two outstanding three-year-olds in Big Game and Sun Chariot, trained by Fred Darling and ridden by Gordon Richards, who were confidently expected to win all the five classics. Big Game duly won the Two Thousand Guineas and Sun Chariot the One Thousand Guineas, and they were installed at odds on for the Derby and Oaks respectively. Arthur Bendir, chairman of Ladbrokes, held the opinion that if Big Game had won the Derby, William would have been unable to settle.

Bendir was not given to making wild statements about his fellow bookmakers but it may be that this opinion was the outcome of wishful thinking. I have no doubt, however, that William was heavily involved over Big Game, and as he told me many years later, he considered himself justified in laying heavily against him, owing to his sprinting pedigree.

To the old-time bookmakers, the horses were of no more significance than the numbers on a roulette wheel. One of them had to come up and the absence of a zero was more than compensated by the prices they then offered being substantially in their favour. William, with his determination to introduce some fun into betting which, incidentally, would ultimately react to his own advantage, was regarded by his colleagues as a gambler who was certain to come to grief. From the turn of the century the bookmaker's sole object had been to be as near overround as possible. This meant that no matter which horse won, he would be a winner.

William, on the other hand, was prepared to lose large sums from time to time, knowing that with his judgment and flair for attracting business, his winning days would far outnumber the days when he was out of pocket. The biggest insult you could pay an old-timer was to suggest he had backed a horse, and William's methods savoured more of those of a punter than a bookmaker, as he made no secret of the fact that he was prepared to stand by his opinion.

William doubted Big Game's ability to stay one-and-a-half miles though the colt had proved himself supreme over a mile. His doubts were well founded, as Big Game's pedigree was decidedly suspect. His dam, Myrobella, was one of the fastest fillies running between the wars and one of the greatest sprinters of her age, but did not stay a yard beyond six furlongs.

Many shared William's doubts concerning Big Game's ability to stay one-and-a-half miles and with two furlongs still to go, Big Game, who had run all too freely, was a spent force and eventually finished fourth. Watling Street, beautifully ridden by Harry Wragg in the colours of Lord Derby, won an exciting race by a neck from Lord Rosebery's Hyperides.

Had Sun Chariot run in the Derby instead of the Oaks, which she won, she would certainly have won, as in the St. Leger she beat Watling Street out of sight.

Sun Chariot was undoubtedly one of the greatest fillies of all time, a view which was shared by William. He took no chances with her when she ran in the St. Leger and was consequently a good winner of the race.

Five years later the racecourse was buzzing with rumours and counter-rumours concerning William's ability to meet his obligations should the screaming hot favourite, Tudor Minstrel, win Gordon Richards his first Derby.

Tudor Minstrel started at 7–4 on, the shortest price at which a horse had gone to post for an Epsom Derby for over half a century. Unbeaten as a two-year-old, Mr. J. A. Dewar's colt had put up a scintillating performance to win the Two Thousand Guineas by eight lengths. He had out-classed his rivals to such an extent that many formed the view the opposition might not be able to get him off the bit, in which case his stamina would not be called upon. His sire, Owen Tudor, had won a war-time Derby and Sansovino, the sire of his dam Sansonnet, had won the Derby by six lengths in hock-deep going. On the other hand, the bottom line of Tudor Minstrel's pedigree was exclusively composed of sprinting blood.

As the horses paraded for the race, the doubt concerning William's ability to settle if the favourite won, monopolised the conversation of those on the tightly packed stand.

William, with his knowledge of breeding, had all along maintained that while Tudor Minstrel was the best miler of the time, he would fail to stay one-and-a-half miles. There was yet another factor in his calculations. For some weeks past, the late Major Mackenzie, then one of the heaviest bettors of the day, had been investing quietly on Blue Train who, like Tudor Minstrel, was trained by Fred Darling. William told Mackenzie that Darling had not backed Blue Train with his firm, or even enquired about his price. "Oh yes he has", replied Mackenzie, inferring that some of the money he had bet on Blue Train was the trainer's. No matter how independent he may be, this is the sort of information a bookmaker cannot ignore. Major Mackenzie was then Managing Director of the Greyhound Racing Association, and a professional backer to boot.

Blue Train was one of the most beautifully bred horses ever to appear on a racecourse. Both his parents were immortals. His sire was Blue Peter, winner of the Two Thousand Guineas and Derby, who would surely also have won the St. Leger had the race been run in 1939, while his dam, Sun Chariot had won the One Thousand Guineas, Oaks and St. Leger.

Somewhat backward, Blue Train had been very lightly raced, but after a fluent victory in the Newmarket Stakes, became a public fancy. Alas, for William's book, ten days before the race, Blue Train broke down and never ran again. There was a precedent for William's fancy for Blue Train, as in 1938 Pasch had won the Two Thousand Guineas, trained by Fred Darling, and started hot favourite for the Derby in which, to the dismay of his backers, he could finish only third. The race was won by his stable companion, Bois Roussel.

Blue Train's absence left Hill with a completely lopsided book with a victory for Tudor Minstrel costing him the best part of £200,000 [now £3,500,000]. Although William was doing great business, Hill House had not yet established itself as the offshoot of the Bank of England, which it subsequently became. Five years later, William's backers need have had no qualms, and it may well be that the widely expressed fears concerning his ability to meet his obligations were groundless. With hindsight, it seems incredible that Big Game and Tudor Minstrel should have started at 6–4 on and 7–4 on respectively and that backers should still have been falling over one another to accept these absurd odds when the races started.

Both horses had been brilliant two-year-olds and even before

Tudor Minstrel made his debut, Gordon Richards had said he was convinced he was the fastest two-year-old he had ever ridden, and he had ridden more 'pigeon catchers' than any man alive. Possessed of terrific initial speed, Big Game and Tudor Minstrel had been encouraged to go like bats out of hell and pulverise the opposition in the first three furlongs, tactics which would prove fatal to a horse's chance in the Derby.

A racehorse is not a very intelligent animal for the very good reason that human beings do all his thinking for him from the day he is foaled. Having been accustomed to jump off and go for his life, a horse can be forgiven if he resents restraint and fights for his head when his jockey tries to drop him out and settle him down in the middle of the field.

Big Game and Tudor Minstrel behaved in their respective Derbys as if they thought Gordon Richards had taken leave of his senses. I don't know how much William could see of the 1947 Derby from his pitch on the rails, but if he had watched it high up on the stand, he would have realised his future was safe before the field had covered half-a-mile. Tudor Minstrel was pulling Gordon's arms out and was racing with his head on one side in an endeavour to get his accustomed position and in the long history of the Derby, the race has never been won by a horse which declined to cooperate with its jockey.

Soon after the war, William's overheads had increased enormously with the growth of his business and his resources were further stretched by his decision to go into ownership in a big way. By this time, only the best was good enough for this increasingly successful young man and he decided to purchase the five-year-old Chanteur II, one of the three best stayers in France. The end of the war found this country bankrupt for stayers, as owners had been discouraged from keeping their horses in training after they were three-year-olds in war time, with the result that there had been very few long distance races. Breeders had therefore concentrated on breeding for speed.

Quintin Gilbey commented on the details of Chanteur II's career:

"In France, under German occupation, racing had been almost back to normal. The Germans considered that recreation would prevent the Parisians from becoming obstreperous and, needless to say, they were intending to appropriate all the best French horses immediately the war was over, and send them to Germany.

In consequence, in the late forties and early fifties, French horses swept the board in our big races over all distances in excess of a mile.

In the Gold Cup of 1946, Chanteur II had finished second to M. Boussac's Caracalla, in Charlie Elliott's opinion, one of the best horses he ever rode.

The other was Pharis in the same ownership. Chanteur II was the property of M. Magot, and was trained at Chantilly by the famous trainer Henry Count, and was sent over to England to contest the Winston Churchill Stakes of 1¼ miles at Hurst Park on Saturday, May 24 and the White Rose Stakes of one mile seven furlongs on the following Monday.

On my arrival at Hurst Park on the Saturday, I met Chanteur II's French jockey Roger Brethes, and from our subsequent conversation I like to think that I may possibly have been in some small way responsible for Hill purchasing this very good horse. Roger Brethes was very worried, as he told me he had never previously ridden over the trappy Hurst Park track and the English jockeys had not been at all cooperative when asked to point out the pitfalls to be avoided.

I had raced regularly at Hurst Park for nearly 30 years, and having walked the course on several occasions, I was able to explain the general lay out of the track. The opposition to Chanteur II was strong and as 1¼ miles was well short of his best distance, I suggested to Brethes that he should set him alight on entering the straight and go for his life. This would obviate any possibility of his being chopped for speed in a false run race. This Brethes did and Chanteur II won comfortably from M. Boussac's Nirgal. On the Monday, over one mile seven furlongs, Chanteur II won as he liked against far weaker opposition. I expect Chanteur II and Brethes would have won the first of these two races without my assistance, but had they not done so I do not think that Hill would have bought Chanteur II.

The horse's objectives were the Coronation Cup, two days before the Derby, and the Gold Cup at Ascot. He was then to be retired to the stud. After Chanteur II had won the Winston Churchill Stakes, Brethes said to me 'one good turn deserves another, and I suggest you have a 'saver' in the Derby on Pearl Diver, the mount of George Bridgland. I know his French form is not very impressive, but he stays well, which your Tudor Minstrel may not do, and he is improving all the time.' I therefore took £80 to £2 and the odds a place about Pearl Diver with Hills, and so despite the fact that I had backed Tudor Minstrel, both before and after the race for the Guineas, I was a winner on the Derby.

Pearl Diver, who never won another race, stormed home by four lengths from the Aga Khan's Migoli, with Sayajirao three-quarters of a length back in third. Tudor Minstrel, who had been out of the race at Tattenham Corner, was a farther eight lengths away back in fourth.

It has been suggested that the 1947 Derby required very little winning. This view was not supported by subsequent events as Migoli went on to beat Tudor Minstrel in the Eclipse Stakes, and the following year won the Prix de l'Arc de Triomphe, while Sayajirao won the St. Leger.

I think it highly probable that Brethes, having marked my card concerning Pearl Diver, passed on similar information to Hill after he had ridden his Chanteur II to victory in the Coronation Cup, in which case Hill must have enjoyed a fabulously successful Derby.

Starting at 3–1 on, Chanteur II won the Coronation Cup by five lengths from M. Boussac's 1945 French Derby winner Coaraze. Hill had only become the owner of Chanteur II a couple of days before the Coronation Cup was run. The deal was concluded (so Hill thought) with M. Magot at an agreed sum of £80,000. [£1,360,000] After winning the race for Hill, Chanteur II was sent back to Henry Count's stable in France to be trained for the Ascot Gold Cup. On arriving in France, the horse was impounded by the Ministry of Agriculture, who forbade the sale to go through unless a further £10,000 [£170,000] was paid. One can imagine the furore there would have been in this country over such ministerial interference.

As the horse had already won a big race in Hill's colours, the latter had no alternative than to pay the extra money. Although Chanteur II failed to win the Gold Cup, Hill never had a moments regret regarding his expenditure of £90,000 as Chanteur II soon proved an outstanding sire.

His first crop of juveniles won 12 races, while his second crop included the mighty Pinza, who provided Sir Gordon Richards (knighted only that week) with his first Derby winner in 1953 after so many years of waiting. To Fred Darling, then on his death bed, went the credit of breeding Pinza.

Chanteur II's defeat in the Gold Cup was inflicted by another French horse, Souverain. There was no disgrace in his defeat as Souverain had proved himself one of the best three-year-olds in France the previous season, and had beaten the French Derby winner Prince Chevalier in the Grand Prix de Paris. As Prince Chevalier went on to run Caracalla to a neck in the Prix de l'Arc de Triomphe, the form was very good indeed. Souverain was owned in partnership by M. Fernand Schmidt and M. Lucien (Lulu) Chataignoux, partners in a Paris restaurant. They were close friends of Hill and Lionel Barber, who had entertained them on their visit to England while they reciprocated by giving Hill a fine time when he made one of his frequent visits to Paris.

Over two miles at Ascot as a three-year-old, Souverain had beaten Airborne, winner of the Derby and St. Leger, so he was unquestionably a world beater.

One way and another, Derby week 1947 was the most hectic in Hill's career. The 'fun' started at Kempton on the Monday, where a young Earl won £60,000 [£1,000,000] from him. After the race for the Derby, the young Earl went up to Hill and said: "Thank God Tudor Minstrel got beaten. Now I shall be able to sleep tonight." Asked by Hill what the hell he meant, the young Earl replied: "If Tudor Minstrel had won, following on the huge price you paid for Chanteur II, everyone knows you would have 'knocked' and I'd have had to whistle for those lovely sixty thousand 'smackers' I won off you at Kempton."

Hill was not amused, but a bookmaker does not lose his temper with a member of the aristocracy who bets in the sums in which this young Earl betted in which, sad to relate, were the last months of his life.

Before I leave the subject of that eventful week in June, 1947, I should like to emphasise that there was never a shred of evidence to support the contention that Hill would not have been able to meet his obligations had Tudor Minstrel won the Derby, and also to put on record that not even the most jealous of his rivals ever again questioned his ability to do so."

Few men knew more about French racing than Quinny Gilbey, who never missed an important race in France from 1946 until he retired nearly 30 years later. He had also lived in France for a time before the war and spoke the 'lingo' fluently.

5

The fact that a bookmaker loses a large bet to one of his clients does not necessarily mean that he has had a bad race. If the bookmaker realises that it is 'hot' money and the price is in favour of the backer, he will 'hedge' at least part of the bet, and may even back it himself. It is highly probable that only a small proportion of the £60,000 won by the young Earl from William was his own money, while it is very possible that William may have turned round and backed the horse himself.

The bet was made by Jack Green, who was at that time employed by William. Green's duties were multifarious, and included entertaining William's current girlfriends when the guv'nor was otherwise engaged possibly touting jockeys and one way and another discovering what was fancied and what was not. As Green worked commissions for one or two very shrewd stables, and was not above betting for jockeys, he was a valuable member of William's entourage. He also acted as court jester, and was one of William's travelling companions when he went racing in Paris and Deauville. William relied largely on his own knowledge of form, breeding and intuition. Who does not prick up his ears when he hears that a horse is thought to be a certainty by its trainer? Or, alternatively, that it isn't fancied. Green was very well informed on such matters.

By the early fifties, William was on his way having become a millionaire and could afford to dispense with the services of the Greens of this world, although information of the right kind cannot be ignored, no matter how rich a man may be. In the twenties, soft-spoken, white haired Harry Slowburn was the doyen of the ring. One of the most highly respected men on the Turf, he was nevertheless known to be the best informed bookmaker in the ring, though no one had any idea how he obtained his information. All the 'heads' betted with him and this fact alone stood him in good stead. No big bookmaker minds losing to the well-informed as their bets supply him with information concerning the horses backed by them.

Jockeys are well known to be bad tipsters, but bookmakers have nevertheless bought information from them. There were two jockeys suspected of being in the hands of bookmakers around this time and, sorry to say, one committed suicide while the other died almost destitute. I am not suggesting that bookmakers were to blame, as both men were compulsive gamblers.

Just as the late 1920's could be described as the 'golden age' of jockeyship with Steve Donoghue, Gordon Richards, Brownie Carslake, Joe Childs, Harry Wragg, Charlie Elliott, Charlie Smirke, Michael Beary and Tommy Weston, so could the years 1945–1950 be described as the most flourishing age for racecourse bookmakers. Those who had stayed at home during the war had made fat profits, while those who had served overseas had their gratuities and pensions. For over six years there had been little on which to spend money, and although the bare necessities of life, much less luxuries, were still in short supply for several years after the surrender of Germany, it was only natural that those who had been deprived of the recreation they loved best for so long should flock to our racecourses.

"Who would not be a bookmaker now that peace is here?", a punter remarked to William following the defeat of a hot favourite. William, ever reluctant to admit he had enjoyed a winning day, had to admit, somewhat grudgingly, that he was doing quite nicely thank you.

Other big bookmakers of the time were Albert Williams, Willie Preston, who had been in the game since he was a boy of 18, and was later to work for William after his retirement as a course bookmaker, Laurie Wallis, Maxie Parker, Hector Macdonald, Jack Burns, Jack Wilson, Charlie Hunter Simmonds, Percy Thompson, Ladbrokes with whom it was possible to win or lose a fortune.

It will be appreciated by 1948 that although Hill had become number one bookmaker, he had plenty of opposition. The Ladbrokes of that day was still then the property of Arthur Bendir, who had expressed his doubts as to whether William could have met his obligations had Big Game won the Derby. The firm, under Bendir, bore little resemblance to the huge organisation it has become today; it was a unique organisation with a cosy office in Old Burlington Street and a clientele almost exclusively composed of 'mug punters' from the higher strata of society, nearly all of whom settled their accounts in the long run, though in some cases it was a very long run indeed. Bendir was a very patient man, realising that his aristocratic patrons could not afford *not* to pay him, so his bad debts were negligible.

Few of Ladbrokes clients betted heavily, though many of them did in sums they could ill afford to lose. Bendir, however, would lay a very big bet when the spirit moved him and his most precious possession was a framed cheque for £100,000 [£3,200,000] paid to Mr. Macomber after the American millionaire had brought off the autumn double with Forseti and Masked Marvel in 1925. It was said that Bendir would be reluctant to post a certain young subaltern in the Brigade of Guards, who owed him a large sum of money, knowing that the poor chap would have no alternative than to shoot himself if he did. The shame of being a defaulter would be too great for him to bear. At one time, Ladbrokes had three representatives betting on the rails, two of whom were unique.

Lord Graves, 'Tommy', who was the first peer to bet in Tattersalls' Ring and Mrs. Vernet, the first lady to do likewise. Tommy Graves was a charming person and very popular. Bendir said he was a poor bookmaker but a wonder at introducing new customers. Tommy and the other male members of the firm wore top hats and morning coats when betting at Ascot or Epsom. Mrs. Helen Vernet was always dressed in the height of fashion.

One would imagine that any bookmaker would have given his eye teeth to have secured this gold mine and following Bendir's death in the 1950's when the firm came on the market, it could have been bought by William for a mere £225,000 [£3,825,000]. He let it slip through his fingers, however, and it was one of the biggest mistakes of his life. He is alleged to have said that he did not want to be bothered with so many small accounts, apparently oblivious to the fact that a client who loses £100 and pays, is a better business proposition than one who loses £1,000 and is never heard of again.

William's loss was Maxie Parker's gain. Maxie Stein, under the name of Maxie Parker, had made a successful book for a number of years, as had his brother Harry Parker, known on every racecourse as 'Snouty.' There were two other brothers, Jack and Isaac. Jack had a brilliant young son called Cyril. When Maxie died, he left his recent purchase to his nephew Cyril Stein and all the world knows that he has built up the firm so that it not only is at least on an equal footing with Hills, but has branched out far and wide.

Cyril Stein is the exact antithesis of William Hill. He never betted on the racecourse, but is acknowledged to possess one of the best financial brains in Europe. The accounts which he took over from the Bendir Organisation he placed in the hands of Dickie Gaskell, a man of great charm, who not only retained the clients he inherited from Bendir, but added to their number.

William described himself as a 'dissenter' in that he seldom accepted the views and decisions of others and the following are two examples of his perversity. In the early fifties, a jumper named C.D.B. won at a holiday meeting at Huntingdon at 25–1. As there were fifteen or more meetings on that day, it was not possible for *The Sporting Life* or *The Sporting Chronicle* to have one of their regular starting price representatives at the meeting, and it was left to a comparatively inexperienced staff man from the office to return the SP's. Taking advantage of this, one or two bookmakers at the meeting organised a skilfully planned starting price coup by placing their money in the office and extending the odds on the racecourse, both visibly on their boards and vocally by means of a repetition of '25–1 C.D.B.' at the top of their voices. The correct price should have been in the region of 6–1. The horse won and at the subsequent enquiry the London Advertising Bookmakers' Investigation Committee agreed that all bets should be ratified, despite the obvious absurdity of the price. This was done to maintain confidence in a system which had been in existence for over 100 years. William, however, took the opposite line, declaring that the price had been manipulated, which of course it had, though there is nothing actually dishonest in the racecourse practice of 'knocking out a horse' and backing it at starting price, hoping that the money will not be returned to the course.

It is difficult to see on what grounds William refused to pay as the transaction, although coming into the category of 'decidedly hot' did nothing to infringe the rules of betting. His resentment was that of a man who hated 'being had for a mug', but he eventually relented and everyone was paid. He could hardly do otherwise as a few years earlier he had been responsible for just such a coup.

A year or two later, the opposite occurred. This was in May, 1953 with what came to be known as the 'Francasal Case' which ended up with half-a-dozen men being prosecuted at the Old Bailey and receiving heavy sentences. This was sheer Nat Gould stuff and proves that every now and then the truth really can be stranger than fiction.

A French-bred horse called Francasal won a minor race at Bath, but it subsequently transpired that the winner was not the moderate Francasal but a much better horse of similar colouring called Santa Amaro. All the commissions had been executed at starting price by those in the know. All the telephone lines with Bath racecourse were severed by the gang in order to prevent any money returning to the course from the offices, which would have shortened the price. Not a penny was seen in the ring for the horse called Francasal and he was returned at 10–1, having run out a very easy winner.

Again the Bookmakers' Committee met in London, and very properly told their members this time *not* to pay, as criminal proceedings were being taken. William again took the opposite line and announced that he would pay all clients in full over Francasal, which he did.

One can only assume that those who were paid by William were those who subsequently appeared in the dock at the Old Bailey.

This was an extraordinary decision by William as there could be no question that the money won from him over Francasal had been acquired by one of the most dastardly coups in the history of racing.

It may be of interest to readers for me to explain in detail the origin of starting price betting and the method by which starting prices are compiled.

On race days in the 1880's, bookmakers used to congregate illegally in Hyde Park and bet off home-made blackboards and lists of prices affixed to trees. Before they had been betting for very long, they were moved on by the police. They therefore started using clubs, pubs and dens in Fleet Street, where a number of journalists were frequenters and as these were for the most part private premises, they were not breaking the law. Journalists used to publish reports of the business which went on, and it became convenient for clients to settle their accounts weekly instead of immediately. By agreement with the book-makers and the sporting press, so called 'returns' were made by the journalists and published in their respective papers.

The first full starting price return in a national daily newspaper was published by *The Evening News* in 1883, whose editor at that time was the notorious Frank Harris, friend of all the literary giants of the day, and author of the best seller *'My Life And Loves'*. The circulation of *The Evening News* was trebled within a short time of the starting prices being printed in full.

By 1926, the only sporting papers which remained were *The Sporting Life* and *The Sporting Chronicle*† and, ever since, all starting prices have been returned by the representatives of these two papers.

No praise is too high for these men, and no one appreciated more fully the admirable manner in which they carry out their arduous task than William Hill. On every day on which racing takes place, these men from *The Sporting Life* and *The Sporting Chronicle* are responsible for the turnover of millions of pounds. When one realises that half a point either way can make the difference nowadays of £500,000 to a firm of the magnitude of Hills or Ladbrokes, one appreciates how accurate they must be. We all know the old cliche about it being impossible to please everyone, but Geoffrey Hamlyn and his colleagues achieved the impossible six days a week, and it is not more than once or twice a year that one hears either a backer or a bookmaker question the accuracy of the starting prices.

---

† *The Sporting Chronicle* went out of business in 1985, and 'reps' of the Press Association now officiate with *The Sporting Life*.

6

The year 1949 was a season of real racecourse drama for William. All the world knows that he bred a Derby winner after only six years in the business of breeding bloodstock, but it is not generally known that the victory of Nimbus, whom he first saw as a tiny foal at his Whitsbury Stud, cost him a fortune.

Nimbus, ridden by Charlie Elliott, had previously won the Two Thousand Guineas by a short-head from the hot favourite Abernant, but William doubted his ability to stay the Derby course, as he was out of a mare called Kong, who had never won over more than six furlongs and had won the Wokingham Stakes at Ascot with the proverbial postage stamp on her back. In 1943, at the dispersal sale of the late Sir Charles Hyde's stock, William, through Phil Bull, had purchased the seven-year-old mare Kong for only 710 guineas. Although she had won only sprint races, she was quite stoutly bred and as he had a nomination to Nearco, the leading sire in this country, William sent Kong to Nearco and the result was Nimbus.

Although Nimbus proved himself a good class two-year-old, William did not visualise him as a potential Derby winner, and even after his victory in the first classic, he still doubted his ability to stay one-and-a-half miles. Charlie Elliott, however, was confident that he would do so, and in the absence of Nimbus' trainer George Colling, he was largely responsible for the colt's preparation. He was certainly in the best position to know. Colling was very ill at the time, and died soon after at an early age.

Notwithstanding Elliott's assurance that Nimbus would get the trip, William continued to lay him, and went for a good win over the French horse Amour Drake, the mount of Rae Johnstone in the colours of the glamorous late Madame Leon Volterra. [known by the press as 'Susie' much to her fury] The race is best described in William's own words:

"Normally I never get excited watching a race. That's the way I'm built. Excitability is a luxury a bookmaker cannot afford. There was, however, one race I watched when all my good resolutions went to the winds. That was the day when Nimbus won the first photo-finish Derby. I can, I think, be excused my excitement as I had a special interest. I bred Nimbus. Actually, I had another interest, but I forgot all about that at the time.

In the Derby, one likes to see the horse in which one is interested nicely placed as the horses gallop down the hill to Tattenham Corner. But it is not until after the horses turn for home that the race really begins to take shape. But Nimbus had led all the way and was on the rails turning into the straight with Lord Derby's Swallow Tail in close attendance. The rest of the field were several lengths behind them. Thus, they came thundering up the straight neck and neck. But they had given all they had and were rolling with fatigue like a couple of drunken sailors holding each other up, or so it seemed.

Then, out of the pack came Amour Drake, the French horse I thought was a certainty, but as he approached the two leaders with only 100 yards to go, they veered over to the centre of the course. Rae Johnstone, on Amour Drake, was faced with a problem. Should he carry on and run the risk of being bored out towards the rails of the Members' enclosure, or check his mount and challenge between the leaders and the far rails. He decided to snatch up his mount and challenge on the far side. The manoeuvre cost Amour Drake a couple of lengths and the race for, as luck would have it, Nimbus and Swallow Tail straightened up and had he challenged on the stands' side, he would not have been impeded. The three horses passed the post in line, but the photograph showed that Nimbus had won by a head from Amour Drake, with Swallow Tail a neck away third. A stride past the post, Amour Drake was in front.

When Nimbus's number went into the frame, I vaulted the rails and, within seconds, I was in the winner's enclosure. There were, of course, congratulations for the owner Mrs. Glenister to whose husband I had sold Nimbus for 5,000 guineas as a birthday present, and the jockey Charlie Elliott, who had ridden such an enterprising race. My private pride and jubilation was something no one could share – I had bred a Derby winner.

You cannot put a price on that thrill, but the following day I woke up with a victory hangover that few men in a moment of triumph have ever had to face. Winning the race had provided Mrs. Glenister with the then record prize of £14,245, [£242,165], but Nimbus's victory had cost me £200,000 [£3,400,000]. You see, I had backed Amour Deake to win me that sum, but what did that matter now? To a man really interested in horses and in breeding bloodstock, there is no thrill in the world to match the sheer joy of breeding a Derby winner."

This was the era of the big gambler and for the first time in racing history, two of the biggest backers were ladies – Miss Dorothy Paget and Mrs. J. V. (Pat) Rank. James de Rothschild had long been famous for his spectacular tilts at the ring, and from time to time he would still bet in huge sums. Every generation produces one or two individuals who will attempt to break the bank in Tattersalls' ring, but no one has yet succeeded.

In the late forties and early fifties, William was the right man at the right time in the right place. He had the form of every runner at his fingertips, and armed with this knowledge and an adequate supply of the right kind of information, he was prepared to take £30,000 or £40,000 [£500,000] *a race* at any big meeting, whilst he was heavily committed in every big ante-post race. By this time, every one of any note in the racing world had an account with William, and while some of his colleagues fought shy of the top professionals, who annually made a good living out of backing horses, William welcomed their business as it gave him an additional line to the prospects of the fancied horses. Just because a bookmaker lays a big bet, it does not mean that he is stuck with it. Many professional backers succeed in beating the book for a number of years, but few of them manage to hang on to it.

One exception, however, was Tom Westhead who died in January, 1966, at the age of 82, and left over £100,000 [£800,000]. This cloth-capped Lancastrian was a bookmaker himself in the 1920's and turned professional backer in 1930. He also owned several good horses. He won the Cesarewitch in 1937 with Punch, having backed him to win with over £50,000 [£1,600,000]. He was no rash gambler and based his betting on a thorough knowledge of form, plus a first-class intelligence service as to what was gong on in the various stables, many of whom entrusted him with their commissions. Although Hill was a bookmaker, and Westhead was a backer, it will be appreciated that they employed similar means to achieve their end.

I have devoted some space to this hard-headed professional who was one of several, in order to illustrate the strength of the opposition William and the other leading bookmakers had to contend with and to dispel the view held by so many non-racing people that all backers are pushovers.

By 1950 the post-war boom was nearly over and the money began to dry up. The bookmakers could not complain about this as the Spring Double was landed by Dramatic and Freebooter and every bookmaker lost money in the first week of the season. Had betting been on the same scale as in the previous five years, they would have lost a fortune. It was by far the most expensive Double since the war, and Alex Bird, professional backer who died at the end of 1991, was reported to have won £150,000 [£1,950,000].

William paid out his share of the general losses, but won money over the Derby and Oaks, though they were won by well fancied horses in Galcador and Asmena, both carrying the colours of M. Boussac. The fact that he showed a profit when these races were won by horses in the forefront of the market, testifies to his judgment of form and the ability to assess a horse's potential stamina. For the past five years horses owned by M. Boussac had ruled the roost, and never in living memory had one owner won so many great races in England and France in so short a space of time. William had been prepared for Boussac's successes, was very rarely a loser when one of Boussac's horses were successful, no matter at what price it had started.

William had fielded against the hot favourite Prince Simon and would have been a heavy loser had he won. He came very near to doing so, but having held a long lead he was caught close home by Galcador, whose success compensated Rae Johnstone for his unlucky defeat on Amour Drake. Harry Carr was unfairly criticised for his riding of Prince Simon. The Press were almost equally divided as to whether he had made sufficient use of Prince Simon's stamina or whether he had ridden him into the ground. As it was obvious not all his critics could be right, one or two were correct in describing him as having ridden a perfect race. This was the view of Prince Simon's trainer, Captain Cecil Boyd-Rochfort.

M. Boussac and his jockey Rae Johnstone went on to win the St. Leger with Scratch II and although he started second favourite at 9–2, William again had a winning race, as Scratch II had previously won the French Derby.

M. Boussac's last big triumph in this country was with Talma II in the St. Leger in 1955, regarded by William Hill as the most astonishing race during his career as a bookmaker. Talma II landed a gamble, possibly the biggest of that season, but whose money it was which brought his price tumbling down from 100–6 to 7–1 remains a mystery.

Before racing that day, William began to call over the card in his usual manner, but no one was interested until he mentioned Talma II. "Who wants 1000–60 Talma?" he asked, and bedlam ensued. Voices were raised, hands were outstretched and William and his staff were nearly pushed over the rails in the rush. Shouts of: "I'll have that" . . . "Five times, Bill" . . . "To win three grand" and many more such acceptances. William appeased most of them and laid Talma II to lose the best part of £30,000 [£390,000] at 100–6. Money continued to pour on the French horse and he eventually started second favourite at 7–1.

One can only hazard a guess as to where the information came from, as even when they fancied a horse, the connections of Talma II never gambled on anything like that scale. M. Boussac's manager, Francois de Brignac, and Rae Johnstone were close friends of William's and he knew that neither of them gave Talma II more than an outside chance. Rae was emphatic that the horse had little speed, but was just the sort to win the Queen Alexandra Stakes the following year at Royal Ascot.

In the paddock before the race, Talma II behaved disgracefully and never before has a classic horse been seen to work himself up into such a state of sexual excitement. He was bathed in sweat, his eyes were staring out of his head and he was still excited when he was mounted and cantered to post. The race was a procession. Nothing could ever get near Talma II and the judge's verdict was a dozen lengths, although it looked more like twenty to most people. If ever a horse should have been tested for dope, that horse was Talma II. This was substantiated when in subsequent races he never ran within two stone of the form he produced on that sensational occasion at Doncaster, though he started favourite in two later Ascot Gold Cups.

To the amazement of the huge crowd, however, the stewards took no action, surely one of the greatest cases of dereliction in the long and honourable history of the Jockey Club. Discussing the race that evening with William, everyone agreed that the most likely explanation for Talma II's outrageous behaviour and subsequent victory was that he had been doped by someone not connected with the stable. It was not suggested that M. Boussac or any of his staff were responsible. But, as William said: "If ever a horse was doped, that horse was Talma II and I will carry that conviction to my dying day."

In 1951, William realised that racecourse business had dropped so alarmingly that his presence on the racecourse was no longer necessary or even desirable. He went on betting on the rails until the middle of 1955, but by then was only operating on Saturdays, when there was still plenty of money about, although he still betted at the big meetings, such as Epsom and Ascot. There had been an economic crisis, and rumours of further devaluation of the pound made both backers and bookmakers more careful with their money than they had been in the previous five years.

The year 1953 provided a most intriguing Derby situation. On the one hand, there was H.M. The Queen's Aureole, backed by millions of loyal stay-at-home punters, and on the other hand, the giant Pinza, who was confidently expected to provide Gordon Richards with his first Derby winner. And so it proved.

Two years later, at Ascot in 1955, William finally quit the racecourse. The truth was that he had become too big to fit into its contracting pattern. The pinch had begun to be felt, and the presence of a man offering £50,000 to £10,000 the field at a run-of-the-mill meeting was neither necessary nor (from the firm's point of view) desirable.

7

By the end of 1942 William's office business had increased so rapidly that it became necessary to separate the football business from the racing business, both for physical reasons, and as a matter of financial expedience. Clients were still sending bets, both on racing and football, in ready money through the post, and as this was at that time illegal, all such bets were void and the money had to be returned.

It was for this reason that William Hill (Glasgow) Limited was formed and within a few months the football business was almost as big as the racing. The Fixed Odds coupon had become so popular that it was issued both from Glasgow and the new London company known as William Hill (Football) Limited in Ludgate Circus. This allowed the Park Lane staff, now numbering over 100, to concentrate on racing, but with the boom years now in full swing, another move soon became necessary.

This time it was to the middle of Piccadilly Circus, in the building which had previously been the Winston Hotel. A vast reorganisation of the building was necessary, and Hill ran into trouble with the authorities for exceeding the regulation amount of building alterations and redecorating allowable at that time and was fined £500.

But the work had been done and the old-fashioned hotel transformed into well furnished offices with up-to-date equipment and 200 telephones. During the renovations, the business was thriving and expanding. All turnover records were being broken. The year 1947 was indeed a memorable one for William as his major ventures on the racecourse coincided with the completion of his move to Piccadilly, where the business remained for twelve years.

Between 1947 and 1953, William had to close 15,000 accounts as the administrative facilities were not available to deal with them. This made him sad, as he hated turning away business, and a number of people who would no longer be able to bet with him on credit were acquaintances. But William said at the time, "After six years in Piccadilly, we were once again bulging at the seams." He had now become a national figure in every sense of the word. The transformation from 1939, when he was known to only the habitues of Northolt Park, to being the world's biggest bookmaker was now complete. He was constantly being questioned as to the secret of his success, and what qualities are required to be a national bookmaker. He listed four essentials:

1.) "Integrity. Without doubt integrity is the most important quality.

   Let your client see that he can trust you and that you trust him and always give the client the benefit of the doubt. Nothing is so hard to live down as a bad name, so don't get one.

2.) Ability to assess. A bookmaker is no use if he cannot assess values mathematically. If you misjudge the market value of what you are offering, you will soon be in the red. I make a practice of assessing prices personally – it is something that comes with long experience and the kind of arithmetical mind I happened to be born with.

3.) Courage. It is no good having dreams without the courage to pursue them. A bookmaker owes it to himself and his clients not to go bust, but he has to be more than a book balancer if he wants to rise above the crowd. He has to think fast, decide what risks he is justified in taking, and then give the customers something attractive.

4.) Initiative. The initiative is knowing what the public wants and to give it them in full – value is essential. The British are born gamblers, but they recognise shoddy stock, and any bookmaker who thinks he can take his clients for a ride is asking for trouble."

In December, 1951, Lionel Barber, who had been auditing the firm's accounts since 1939, decided to join the Hill Organisation full time. The Hill Organisation had expanded rapidly during the war, but like every other firm was handicapped by lack of staff, while the Excess Profits Levy had taken away a large proportion of the firm's profits. The firm continued under financial stress – largely, according to Barber, because William was always trying to run when he should have been walking. Barber cites as an example William's purchase of the Whitsbury Stud in 1943 as causing 'financial indigestion.'

Nevertheless, Lionel Barber, with his shrewd financial brain, could see a brilliant future for the firm of William Hill, and towards the end of the war, William Hill (Football) Ltd. and William Hill (Glasgow) Ltd. became separate entities. The Glasgow company was absolutely essential, as punters would keep sending ready money to London. William had been prosecuted for this on two occasions and a further offence would have meant imprisonment.

These two companies and William Hill (Park Lane) Ltd. progressed from year to year, and Barber was constantly in search of a suitable vehicle to deal with the financial side.

In 1954, he was offered Holders Investment Trust Ltd., a small long established Investment Trust company with £55,000 capital – the 2s shares then worth 2s 9d. Arrangements were made to acquire 75 per cent of the issued share capital. This was done through the Stock Exchange at a price of 2s 10d a share. By March, 1955, the Trust Company was able to acquire William Hill (Football) Ltd. for £1,050,000 [£13,650,000] to be paid for by seven annual instalments of £150,000. Holders' shares rocketed. By March, 1956, the genius of Lionel Barber had proved so successful that the Trust Company was able to acquire William Hill (Glasgow) Ltd. for £2,000,000 [£26,000,000].

Within four years, one share in Holders Ltd., bought at 2s 10d was worth ten shares of a value of £18.10s. This tremendous advance in the fortunes of the Organisation was entirely the work of Barber as William, although the greatest racecourse bookmaker of all time, had a very limited knowledge of the world of finance. It had always been the intention to include William Hill (Park Lane) Ltd., but that company owned both the Whitsbury Stud and Sezincote Stud and neither was in any way connected with betting. Hill had always wanted to own these studs personally and he achieved this in July, 1961. As a result, William Hill (Park Lane) Ltd. was sold to the Trust Company for £2,000,000 cash, payable by £1,000,000 down, and the balance in instalments of £200,000.

With his share of the down payment, William was able to acquire the two studs and the group as a whole was not deprived of any liquid resources. The method adopted in bringing the betting business into Holders was the first time a 'shell' company had been so used and many people thought that the Stock

45

Exchange might reject such a transaction. Far from doing so, this method is now given as a model case in text books on accountancy. The fundamental point was the relationship between Barber and Hill as each had a profound respect for the other's ability – one as a bookmaker and the other as a Chartered Accountant. Until 1965, when they parted as a result of William's interference in matters of which he had no expert knowledge, they never had a serious quarrel.

In the mid-sixties, William had over 100,000 credit clients and another 100,000 clients who bet in cash by post. They also had a file of 5,000,000 football clients from whom they received in the Fixed Odds days 2,000,000 coupons per week. All now housed in a new building in Blackfriars Row. The total betting turnover in 1964 was £50,000,000 [£400,000,000]. Every client had his own personal file with every letter he had written to the firm included. One of the key figures in the build-up of William's enormous office organisation was Roy Sutterlin. He joined the Hill Organisation in 1946 on being demobilised from the RAF in which he had served throughout the war as a navigator in coastal command. Hill always referred to him as 'my factory manager.' Roy retired in the mid-eighties, and died in 1992.

Sutterlin recalls that when he started with the Hill organisation in Park Lane there were 30 telephones; in Piccadilly Circus there were 120 rising to 200, and in the new building there were 400 telephones dealing with racing alone. While all these revolutionary changes in London were taking place, William was continuing to make a most successful book on the racecourse, despite the financial stringency which afflicted the country at that time. The following anecdote testifies to his application to duty at the expense of his own convenience and that of his staff.

On the last day of the St. Leger meeting the train for London from Doncaster inconveniently left a few minutes after the last race. Most Londoners, including some bookmakers, ignored the last race which in those days was the Rufford Abbey Handicap over two miles. As usual, William's staff were impatient to be away but, as the horses were going down, a lady owner's secretary (nothing to do with Dorothy Paget or Mrs. Rank), approached William, and asked for a £10,000 bet on her horse. William accepted the wager, told his staff to remain and started his usual display of fireworks. He soon 'bet up' to the horse in question, and indeed, took over £30,000 [£510,000] on the race. The lady's horse was unplaced to the 20–1 winner, and Hill had a 'skinner'. Sauntering off the racecourse, he remarked to his staff, "Wasn't that better than running off to catch the early train."

8

William prided himself on his ability to judge a man's character and the fact that he was successful in securing a staff which combined integrity with efficiency, reveals that this was no idle boast. One of his greatest 'finds' was Peter Blackwell, who joined the Hill Organisation in 1946. Blackwell caught the racing bug at an early age whilst doing a stint in the Von Mittzlaff stable in North Germany in the thirties. His stepfather didn't approve, however, and Peter was packed off to Canada and the States to learn the food business in the Crosse & Blackwell factory. Their main office was in the heart of American racing country in Maryland. This increased Peter's love of racing, although he learnt very little about the food business.

On Peter's return to England in 1939, he saw William Hill in action and, in his own words, 'began to lose money to him.' This he continued to do throughout the war – from Burma, India and Ceylon. He started to accept bets from his brother officers all of which ended up in Hill's book. William obviously had complete trust in this young man's integrity, as the bets often did not arrive at the William Hill offices until several weeks after the results had been decided. As a result of this, Peter Blackwell wrote to William from Burma and suggested that he come and see him after the war was over. William replied that he should come and see him, and he might find a more adventurous and lucrative career for him than selling pickles. Blackwell tells me that William was right in so far that his career has been adventurous!

Peter duly introduced himself to William when his terms of employment were outlined, "Start tomorrow at Goodwood, a pony (£25) a week and a dollar in the pound commission." Peter has since told me,

"I was squashed into a hired Rolls, between some heavy-weights, and off we went – to take the crumbs off the maestro's table at the bottom of the rails. Commissar won the Stewards' Cup, and the Budgett brothers backed it with me. I lost £6,000 [£42,000] on the day, took a 'sharp' bet for some each-way doubles which cost £3,500, and at the end of the day William said 'God almighty, it's a wonder they didn't have the braces off you as well.'

I assumed that it was my first and last day as a bookmaker, and the whole day passed in a complete blur. It seemed to me that I had spent it in a mad house. When we got to London, the guv'nor looked at my book and said: 'Well, that's not too bad, plenty of names down there. They'll give it back. Good night' – and so I was still a bookmaker.

At the end of the day, the boss would take us down to Scott's or the Carlton for a drink. This was expensive as he never had any money on him, and not only did we buy drinks, but he usually borrowed a fiver for his cab home, which probably cost him 10s, so he made a nice profit. With a little knowledge of French, I was usually the treasurer when we went to Paris for the big French races, where we would recoup our losses as he was extremely generous on such expeditions.

There was still plenty of money in the ring and Hill was betting in telephone numbers, £30,000 a race being about normal, and often there was not room for a pin prick on his book, and his clerk would be utterly exhausted at the end of a day's racing!"

Those were the days of the great bookmakers; Willie Preston, Percy Thompson, Jack Burns and many others. The banter between them was tremendous.

Peter Blackwell remembers Hill shouting to Burns, when the latter had declined a bet: "What's the matter, Jack? You can't take it with you." To which Burns replied: "I'm not going yet, Bill." Willie Preston subsequently joined the Hill Organisation and betted for them on the rails after William's retirement from the racecourse. At that time Willie was betting for himself and he and William were deadly rivals. They would bet thousands of pounds against one another, simply and solely on their views. Such transactions had nothing to do with bookmaking.

After Alcide won the Lingfield Derby Trial, the press crowded round Hill and asked him: "What price Alcide for the Derby?" Hill replied, "7–1". Which seemed very generous and Jack Cohen, a great character, challenged Hill with the remark: "And how much to Bill?" "As much as you like, Jack," Hill replied. The press looked at Jack Cohen and the latter answered: "I'll have £70,000 to £10,000 [around £900,000 to £130,000]." This was far more than he really wanted to bet, but he did not want to lose face in the eyes of the press.

A few days later, Alcide was scratched from the Derby as a result of an injury. William, therefore, won £10,000 in one hand without experiencing any qualms, but he nevertheless always maintained that he lost money over his ante-post transactions, and that they merely constituted a shop window for his more serious business.

Blackwell recalls that a Peer of the Realm, who was betting in huge sums, had an agreement with William that settlement of his account should not be made until there was £20,000 owing either way. It so happened that he owed £18,000 when he approached Blackwell, prior to an unimportant race at Newmarket, and asked for a bet of £25,000 to £20,000. William was standing only a few yards away and, having caught Blackwell's enquiring eye, came over and explained to his Lordship that it was only a poor sort of race, so why not just have £5,000 to £4,000. As it happened, the horse was unplaced and the young man was profuse in his thanks to William for putting the brake on him.

Blackwell can remember seeing William showing emotion on a racecourse on only two occasions. The first being when Nimbus, bred by him, won the Derby when the excitement was so great that he climbed over the rails into the Members' enclosure on his way to greet the winner, and the second was at Royal Ascot. After four races on the last day, he was losing £85,000 [£1,105,000], but he bet on the last two races as if there was no such thing as settling day. Rank outsiders won the last two races and William went home a winner on the day. As he got into his car, he uttered two words, "Thank God."

On one visit to Paris, the fun had been fast and furious, and very late one night at the Nouvelle Eve, famous for its scantily clad hostesses and dancers, William turned to his then girlfriend and remarked, "I can't think why I brought you along." The brunette was well capable of taking care of herself, and no matter whether it was in a restaurant or a dress shop, she always seemed to choose the most expensive wares.

Peter Blackwell was the treasure for this trip, and William told him he had given the brunette £700 [£10,000], which he hoped would pay the hotel bill and leave change. When Peter went in search of her, she was nowhere to be found. Eventually she returned, weighed down with parcels, and explained, perhaps unnecessarily, that she had been shopping. "Where's the money Bill gave you for the hotel bill?", Peter asked her. "He never said a word about a bill," she replied. "It's true he gave me a few francs to buy myself some presents, but that's all."

William was furious when he heard about it, although the situation was less serious than it would have been for most of us if we found ourselves in Paris without the wherewithal to settle our hotel bill. William had plenty of French contacts and the money was soon forthcoming, but he refused to speak to the brunette on the flight home.

At customs, the brunette had quite a sizeable sum in duty to pay on the 'few francs' worth of presents she had bought herself, and when this little matter had been settled, the customs official asked. "What about that mink coat you're wearing?" The brunette explained, quite truthfully, that it was not new, and that she had worn it on the outward journey. The official turned to William for confirmation and, without batting an eyelid, he announced that he had never seen the coat until that morning, and then stalked out and into his waiting Rolls Royce and drove back to Hill House – all of which goes to prove that no matter who you were, you had to get up very early in the morning to get the better of my brother William.

History does not relate how long it took the brunette to convince the customs official that her mink coat had not been purchased over the weekend, but she was a resilient young woman, well aware on which side her bread was buttered, and a few days later all was forgiven. Although he enjoyed the bright lights and, on rare occasions would stay up to all hours at restaurants and night clubs, William realised he had a very weak head and drank very little. No one ever saw him the least bit worse for wear, and no matter how late it was, he was always in possession of all his faculties.

Peter Blackwell relates how, on one occasion, William took his dinner party on to Churchill's night club in Bond Street. As usual, William had no money on him and on arrival borrowed £50 from the club's boss, Harry Meadows. Many hours later, when the bill was presented, William announced, "It's wrong – they've put ten per cent on it." Peter explained that that was the service charge, to which William replied, "I understand that, but I'm damned if I'm going to pay ten per cent on the £50 I borrowed from Harry Meadows!"

Everyone I have spoken to who worked with William, speak of him with admiration, respect and affection and agree that there has never been anyone like him and never will be again. This does not mean that they were blind to his faults. His personality drew men to him, and like a few football managers, he had the ability to instil the team spirit into his employees, with the result that they gave him all they had. No one needed to be coerced, and I can find no record of anyone being sacked for lack of effort. Unaccountably, he had one deficiency in dealing with those under him, which can only be described as a mental block – he was quite incapable of saying 'well done.'

Everyone likes praise, and stands taller as a result of it. Most bosses take pleasure in telling a man he has done a good job but no matter how well a man had done, William always gave the impression that he thought he could have done a whole lot better. On the other hand, provided William was satisfied a man had done the job to the best of his ability, he did not tear him off a strip, even though his labours had cost the firm money.

Roy Sutterlin recounts that when the move from Piccadilly Circus to the mammoth building in Blackfriars took place, it was completed in twenty-four hours. It was a tremendous job and no one put more physical effort into it than William. When the last file had been put in its place, he told his staff that he was taking them all to the Dover Castle for a drink. True to form, when the bill appeared, William found he only had a few shillings. History does not relate who paid the bill, but I like to think that whoever it was reimbursed himself on his expense account. No one can tell me why William never carried any money on him, but as he was seldom alone, it cannot be that he was in fear of being robbed.

This seems to be a characteristic common to rich men, two of the richest being the Aga Khan and his son Prince Aly Khan. Both were generous where big sums of money were concerned, but over small sums were positively niggardly. People have seen the Aga Khan debate whether to give his caddy half-a-crown or two bob a few weeks after giving Rae Johnstone the entire stake for winning the Grand Prix de Paris on his My Love. Few rich men understand petty cash, though this could not apply to William Hill, who had known what it was to be very poor indeed.

Prince Aly Khan was a very bad settler. He had no intention of knocking his bookmaker and would pay up when it suited him, but it might take him a year or more. William eventually became fed up with Aly's disregard for the numerous accounts rendered, so when he met the Aga Khan at some social gathering, he mentioned, as tactfully as he could, that Aly owed him money and had done for a considerable time.

The sum was in the neighbourhood of £7,000 [£91,000]. William found this infuriating as only a week before Aly incurred this loss, William had paid him a similar amount. The Aga's reaction to this was to gaze at William reproachfully through his very strong spectacles, and say, "Do you mean to tell me, Mr. Hill, that you are foolish enough to accept bets from my son? You should know better than that."

William eventually ran Aly to earth, and the latter promised to have a cheque ready for him if he would send a messenger to collect it at the Ritz Hotel at 9 o'clock the following morning. The messenger duly arrived on the dot and was told that Prince Aly would be down in a few minutes. After waiting several hours, the messenger asked George, the hall porter, who also carried out the duties of social manager to both the Aga and Aly Khan, when Aly would be available, only to be told that His Highness had left by the back door an hour ago.

With Aly's disappearance down the back stairs at the Ritz, William's patience was at an end and he posted him before Tattersalls' Committee. Bets are not recoverable by law, but if either a backer or bookmaker defaults, the aggrieved part 'posts' him. The case is heard by Tattersalls' Committee, which is composed of men of the highest integrity on both sides of the Rails. If the debt is proved and payment not forthcoming the defaulter is debarred from all racecourses, which is the equivalent of being 'warned off', a great disgrace. Aly settled and the case was never heard.

From a very early age, Aly Khan had three ambitions: to make Casanova look like a selling plater, to own the best horses in the world, and to break the bookmakers. He succeeded in the first, came near to accomplishing the second, and failed lamentably in the third. A bookmaker was fair game in Aly's eyes, and he would not hesitate to employ all the tricks of the trade in order to get the better of him.

In the 1959 One Thousand Guineas, Lester Piggott made one of his rare blunders in electing to ride Collyria in preference to Aly's filly, Petite Etoile, though their trainer, Noel Murless, had little doubt that Petite Etoile was the better. Consequently Doug Smith came in for a lucky chance ride on Petite Etoile.

Before the race, Aly went up to William and said: "Of course Lester Piggott will win – but I'd like a small saver on my filly. What price is she?" "100–8", answered William, to which Aly replied, "Alright, I'll take 1000–80 eight times". That was real sharp practice and rankled William for a long time. He did not often agree with his colleagues, but after Aly had put that fast one over on him, he agreed with the bookmakers who referred to His Highness as 'Aly the spiv'. Aly had the same bet with 'Beau' Goldsmith.

Aly won large sums from William and other bookmakers from time to time, but on balance he was a heavy loser. Although he knew all the tricks of the trade, he was not a good bettor in that the shorter the price, the heavier he would bet. Bookmakers got wise to this and would curtail the odds about the horses he was likely to back. So he was continually taking under the odds. He would also chase his losses and at one Royal Ascot meeting this cost him over £100,000 [£1,300,000].

If anything could have conveyed to Aly the folly of his ways, it was the letter from Tattersalls' Committee, informing him that William Hill Ltd. had 'posted' him. Maybe one of his girlfriend's bracelets had to go, but William got a cheque for the full amount within twelve hours, together with a letter humbly apologising for the 'oversight', while I understand that my sister-in-law received three dozen roses.

Aly received a huge allowance from his father, but such was his extravagance that he was always overdrawn. Shortly after his father's death, he owed the casinos at Deauville, Cagnes and Monte Carlo £150,000. According to Quintin Gilbey, a batch of broodmares and a couple of impressionist pictures had to be disposed of to meet that bill.

9

Roy Sutterlin described William to me as the world's best loser, and the world's worst winner. Sutterlin was responsible for the credit side of the business in the office, which in bookmaking parlance is called the 'field book'. Sutterlin, of course, knew the business inside out, but no matter how good a man is at his job in the betting world, there comes a day when everything goes wrong. On one such day, Sutterlin's 'field book' lost £75,000 [£975,000]. Fortunately, it was not a big day or the losses would have been considerably higher. William was a past master at figures and within five minutes of being shown the day's transactions, he turned to Sutterlin and said, "That's alright. I can't see what else you could have done, and had I been in your place, I should have lost just as much".

On the other hand, should one of his representatives, either on the Rails or in the office, have had a cracking good day and expect a word of praise, all he would receive would be criticism – usually that the turnover had not been bigger, insinuating that Peter Blackwell and his clerk, or whoever it was representing the firm on that particular day, had not worked fast enough. Such criticisms were like water off a duck's back to Peter. He knew William's little ways, and in common with all the senior members of the staff, he and the guv'nor were personal friends.

It sometimes seemed that William was more concerned with turnover than with winning, but it is one of the paradoxes of bookmaking that a bookmaker's turnover is higher when he is losing.

If a punter loses £10, that is the extent of the turnover, but if he has £10 on a 5–1 winner, the turnover is £60. There is also a strong possibility that the lucky backer will give that £50 a run, which will further increase the turnover, and it is also within the bounds of possibility that the £50 will return from whence it came.

Although there was never an occasion after the Derby of 1947 when even the most suspicious of minds could have spread a rumour that William had over-finessed himself, there were occasions when he was faced with colossal liabilities should the second leg of a Spring Double (Lincoln and Grand National) or

Autumn Double (Cesarewitch and Cambridgeshire) oblige. Such an occasion was over the Spring Double of 1957. For no apparent reason, a large percentage of William's clients had coupled Babur with Goosander, but no big bookmaker starts worrying until the first leg wins. It so happened, however, that Goosander's price shortened to approximately 7–1 for the National as the result of two sparkling victories. After he had won the second of these races at Haydock Park, he was described in the national newspapers as 'the ideal Grand National type', and became one of the favourites.

After Babur won the Lincoln, it was impossible for William to hedge his bets without incurring heavy losses, so he decided to take a chance and stand the £300,000 [£3,900,000] realising there were thirty fences to be jumped in a race of four miles and 856 yards. Although Goosander was prominent for most of the race, he failed to finish in the first three, but William showed no signs of elation after the race. On the contrary, he complained that he had not taken more money for some of the others which had finished down the course, or not finished at all.

William used to say that his prominent nose was infallible in sniffing out the 'baddies' and that he could smell a prospective 'knocker' a mile away with the result that he incurred relatively few bad debts. He would bet heavily on his own horses and would accept bets on it as he would on any other horse in the race. His most spectacular bet was '66 monkeys' laid him by a big SP firm which, interpreted, means a bet of £33,000 to £500 [£561,000 to £8,500] his filly Vertencia, in the Cesarewitch. Again the year was 1947. After a desperate race, Vertencia was beaten by about six inches. There is a big difference between winning £561,000 and losing £8,500, but William didn't turn a hair.

He would also lay bets which would make the average bookmaker's hair stand on end. One such bet was laid to the trainer Peter Nelson acting on behalf of his patron, the Maharani of Baroda in the Stewards' Cup at Goodwood in 1950. "What price Victorina?", Nelson asked William, and when told the filly was a 20–1 chance, said, "I'll take that to £5,000 each-way". Victorina was unplaced, but she won the race the following year. History does not relate whether the Maharani recouped her losses, but if she did, it was not with William. After he had ceased betting on the Rails, many people thought William had retired, but nothing could have been farther from the truth, though it is possible it would have been better for the firm if he had. All decisions were taken by him, and having made up his mind, he was, in the words of Roy Sutterlin, Peter Blackwell and Sam Burns, all of whom worked with him for many years, as obstinate as a mule.

Nothing that went on in that huge building in Blackfriars escaped his notice, and it is said that he could have performed the job, however humble, of any one of his 2,000 employees. He was chiefly concerned with matters of policy and administration and controlled the market on the big events, just as he had done since the earliest stage of the firm. Even so, there was not enough to occupy his restless energy and his continual presence in the office became something of a liability to his staff, every one of which was perfectly capable of carrying out his job without the assistance of the boss. William was often heard to say, but never within a mile of his office, that the business could run itself with no help from him. This was perfectly true, but he would have been very hurt had anyone had the temerity to agree with him.

William's bitter opposition to betting shops cost the firm several million pounds. Had Barber and Balshaw had their way, Hill's would have gone into the betting shop business as soon as they were legalised. But Hill's stayed out for three or four years before Bill Balshaw finally persuaded William that the firm must purchase betting shops or go bust.

In 1973, Hill's turnover was £140,000,000 [£700,000,000] of which eighty-five per cent came from the firm's 850 betting shops. To those of us who had been backing horses for over fifty years, and never been inside a betting shop, it seems incredible that course betting contributed only 15 per cent to this huge turnover, on course betting now probably accounts for 5% of turnover. I should like to make it clear, however, how important course betting is, not only to the great firms, but to every bookmaker in the land. It is on the course that the starting price is returned, without which their business would be at a standstill.

Although it was impossible for William to say 'well done,' he paid good wages and there was never any industrial disputes in any of his offices. Once a year, William would transport his entire staff to Whitsbury, where they would be entertained lavishly, the best of food and drink being followed by side shows

59

and a cabaret with first class artists organised by his old friend, Chesney Allen.

Business had so monopolised Hill's life that when he became rich and could afford to relax, he found himself with no hobbies. In consequence, he turned his attention to his studs at Whitsbury and Sezincote, and his farm on the Whitsbury estate where his herd of Friesians became famous, and took top prizes at all the leading shows. For the first few years, the farm had lost money, but from the time he installed his nephew, Christopher Harper, as manager, it began to make money. William was delighted that one of the younger generation should have inherited his business acumen.

William had always been interested in politics and I have already mentioned his left-wing sympathies. Communist Harry Pollit was a close friend of his for some years though, I find it hard to believe that William ever shared Pollit's extreme left-wing views. Throughout his life, William described himself as a Socialist, but as is the way with members of that party, when they become rich, they become less and less interested in politics. It was a bitter blow to William when James Callaghan, on becoming Chancellor of the Exchequer, far from removing the 25 per cent tax imposed by Reginald Maudling on fixed odds football betting, increased it to 33 per cent.

William spent his weekends at Whitsbury but he would be in the office by 10.30 am on Monday, although there was little for him to do.

Soon after the war, he and his wife Ivy had gone on a winter holiday to Montego Bay, and both fell in love with Jamaica. There he entertained on a lavish scale, and on his third visit bought the house which had belonged to the Duke of Sutherland. His annual holidays grew longer and longer until he was spending three months in the West Indies. He was in constant touch with his London office, and long before his return to London, was conducting an ante-post market on the Spring Double.

Until William appeared on the scene, all bookmakers had been Conservative, not only politically but in the manner in which they conducted their business. The status quo had to be preserved at all costs, and any bookmaker who expressed the view that the world might be a happier place if its wealth were more evenly distributed, would have been ostracised and described as a 'dirty Bolshie'. William was, not only a rebel in that he was prepared to gamble for high stakes; he was a left-wing rebel. And in the eyes of the bookmaking fraternity, a man couldn't sink much lower than that.

William had been brought up in one of the less savoury districts in Birmingham, and though there is no evidence that he ever went to bed hungry, all around him there were children who did so night after night. He never forgot those hungry children, many of them with no shoes and dressed in rags, and Robin Hood was his boyhood hero. He raged at the way that faceless men, whose only concern was their profits, reduced families to near starvation, and attributed all injustice to those on the right.

It was his belief that for the past 100 years, the left had been the refuge for all those who were not getting a square deal, and it was from that quarter that men and women looked for shelter from the rigours and injustice that flowed from the free play of economic forces. Keir Hardie, and those that came after him, championed the cause of the weak against the strong, he once told me.

I agreed wholeheartedly with his sentiments, but pointed out that it seemed to me that a malady afflicted the body politic when Labour was in power. He agreed that the Labour governments had so far failed to fulfil his expectations, but thought that they would 'come on a ton' with more practice, and that even now they made more sense than the Conservatives.

I told him he was a thoroughly constitutional Robin Hood, in that few men had ever taken so much money from the rich and distributed it so generously to the poor, in the shape of wages and gifts to those in need. He replied that he had never thought of himself in that light, but it was obvious the idea pleased him. In reply to my question as to whether a self-made millionaire was a good advertisement for Socialism, he told me the fact that he had risen from penury to riches made him all the keener that everyone else should have the opportunity to do so.

Equal opportunity for rich and poor alike was what William demanded. He thought that in time this might come about under a left-wing government, but never from the right. He had demonstrated in his early days that he did not think the world owed him a living, and was often heard to say that we get out of life what we put into it. What infuriated him, though, was that by the accident of birth, the sons of the rich were automatically entitled to the plum jobs, while those who had been born in the Birmingham slums were doomed to spend their days performing the most menial tasks.

In his formative years, *Das Capital* had been his Bible, and he freely admitted his admiration for Karl Marx as the protagonist of the working man in his fight against the injustices of sweated labour under foul conditions, following the industrial revolution.

10

Apart from Winston Churchill's ill-fated attempt to introduce a betting tax in 1926, which was repealed within a year as unworkable, and the Act of 1928 which introduced Totalisator betting in British racing three years later, politics played little part in Turf affairs prior to the Second World War.

The Totalisator, with the then minimum stake of 2s [10p] was particularly attractive to women, as few bookmakers would have accepted such small bets. The bookmakers naturally resented the competition from the Totalisator, though the majority of the business conducted with it would have held little appeal for them. Things soon returned to normal, but in 1955 a movement was started towards the abolition of bookmakers and a Tote Monopoly.

Various members of the Jockey Club were lobbying Tory MP's on the subject of a Tote Monopoly and the bookmakers were apprehensive of the outcome. In the bookmakers' opinion, the Jockey Club members were only interested in increased remuneration by way of prize money for owners and breeders and were not interested in an improvement in the amenities for the public. Prize money, in countries in which bookmakers had been outlawed, was many times higher than in Britain. But those who advocated a Tote Monopoly did not appear to realise that as in the case of all nationalised industries (which is what a Tote Monopoly would represent) the charge would inevitably be passed on to the public – and that Tote deduction of as much as 30 per cent would soon be the order of the day. They are virtually that now anyway.

A highly controversial debate was initiated in the House of Lords by the late Viscount Astor on June 27, 1956. In his speech, Lord Astor said: "The best thing for horse racing would be a monopoly of the Totalisator. The Tote has no temptation to corrupt jockeys and employees of the Tote Board do not engage in gang warfare. Any Chief Constable would agree that the bookmaker was the main cause of corruption of the police. Bookmakers tend to associate with people engaged in crime because a large amount of money passed through their hands and they could afford to finance other forms of crime as well. There was a borderline between betting and crime, which all interested in law and order would be delighted to see finished by the establishment of a Tote Monopoly, which had proved so successful in other countries."

During the course of the debate, their Lordships, while not wholly agreeing with Lord Astor, appeared to take the view that there was much in what he said, and no speaker was wholeheartedly in favour of the bookmakers. Lord Astor's remarks about the Chief Constables were particularly outrageous.

Winding up for the Government, the late Lord Mancroft, Under Secretary at the Home Office, said: "Of late, the Government has been a little out of love with bookmakers as a class, though I am not going to launch an attack on the profession. There are a number of decent, honourable men in it. But there is an increasing number of crooks and thugs, and it is noticeable that in recent regrettable affrays in London and other big cities, time after time when a man is apprehended, he gives his profession as 'Commission Agent' or 'Turf Accountant.' There is no getting away from the fact that a large number of bookies are responsible for, or behind, or connected with some form of crime."

Naturally, this debate started a flood of Press comment and the following statement by the National Bookmakers' Protection Association: "Their Lordships would have been more helpful if they had paid more attention to facts and thrown less mud. The deplorable attempt to associate bookmakers with gang warfare, prevailing at the present time, was a gigantic red herring produced deliberately to obscure the true purpose of the debate. To damn the bookmaking profession because the gangsters choose to describe themselves as bookmakers is like condemning all women who follow the respectable occupation of actress or model because the 'call girl' elects to describe herself as actress or model when in the witness box. Peers, who act as stewards of the Jockey Club, could have convinced their colleagues that the bookmakers' organisations have been the most powerful influence in cleansing the racecourses of undesirables. In company with the racecourse personnel, who are appointed by the Jockey Club, the bookmakers' organisations rigidly control bookmakers, and those whose conduct is open to question are immediately called to account."

Interviewed by the Press, William made a moderate statement in which he said. "We have been for some time in negotiation with the Jockey Club in an effort to find a method whereby we can get some kind of revenue from starting price bookmakers. We do not want to pay the treasury; we want to collect a levy from anybody who makes his living by bookmaking for the benefit of the racing industry, which means that the public will benefit as well as the owners."

Archie Scott, an old Etonian, who subsequently became the acknowledged leader of the bookmakers in all their dealings with the Government, wrote the following letter to *The Times*: "In the debate in the House of Lords, Lord Astor made very serious allegations against bookmakers. He went so far as to say, 'Because a large amount of money passes through their hands, bookmakers can afford to finance other forms of crime as well.' This infers that bookmaking is, in itself, a crime, a fact which I learnt for the first time. If Lord Astor's object was to further the idea of a Totalisator Monopoly it would have been fairer to hold to strictly financial facts, and not by the introduction of stories of gang warfare and crime in order to prejudice the Government and the public against the bookmakers. Lord Mancroft stated, quite correctly, that in the affrays in London and big cities, time after time when a man was apprehended, he gave his profession as a 'Turf Accountant.' I am quite certain that if these men had been asked to produce their books in support of their claim – that they were bookmakers – not one of them would have been able to do so. I think the time has come for those in high places to cease from putting a slur on members of the profession whose very existence depends on the honour of one man's word against another's, and which, without honour on the side of the bookmaker, would have died with the advent of the Totalisator 30 years ago."

The part played in the William Hill Story by Archie Scott, who died in September, 1965, deserves some elaboration. For nine years, he and William were increasingly together and they played a leading part in all the negotiations between the bookmakers, the Jockey Club and the Government, which led to the Betting and Gaming Act of 1960 and Betting Levy Act of 1961. Archie Scott was loved by all who knew him, which can rarely be said of a man, least of all a bookmaker.

Born in 1904 and educated at Eton and Cambridge, Scott was destined for the City, but soon found that way of life intolerable. He had spent a lot of his undergraduate days at Newmarket and decided to try and earn his living on the Turf. He made his first appearance in 1928 as clerk to the late Sydney Fry, the ex-amateur billiards champion, and in 1933 Archie joined the late Dick Fry in partnership, and the firm Scott-Fry was represented at all the major meetings. The partnership lasted until the outbreak of war, when Archie Scott was commissioned in the Green Howards. He served overseas throughout the war and contracted rheumatic fever in the western desert from which he never really recovered, and his health was permanently undermined.

In 1961, the business was taken over by Alfred Cope and eighteen months later Cope's vast racing business was merged with William Hill's. Thus, the two most influential bookmakers of their day were housed under the same roof. Scott's work behind the scenes on behalf of the bookmakers was immense, and in the post war years, he devoted more of his time to committee work on behalf of the bookmaking fraternity than to his own business.

In 1937, Archie married the Hon. Ruth Dawnay, the only daughter of Viscount Downe. She was killed in a car accident near Newmarket in the autumn of 1962. In April, 1965, his second son, Ian, was killed on active service in Aden.

Archie never recovered from these two shattering blows. His health had been a matter of deep concern to all his friends for a number of years, as it was known that he had a heart condition which might prove fatal at any time. When he died tributes were paid him from every quarter of the racing world.

Major-General Sir Randle Feilden, Chairman of the Turf Board, said, "He was a close personal friend since our school days at Eton, and later at Cambridge. My colleagues and I are grateful to him for the contributions he made to racing and to the part he played with the Levy Board."

Field-Marshal Lord Harding, then Chairman of the Levy Board, and Sir Alexander Sim, then Chairman of the Totalisator Board, paid tribute to his negotiating ability, while *The Financial Times'* correspondent considered that Archie Scott did more to maintain the reputation of his profession than any man, and in the opinion of that paper was solely responsible for averting a

Tote Monopoly: "His integrity", wrote their correspondent, "was a by-word on the racecourse, and, in addition, he was a man of great personal charm".

But it is only right and proper that William Hill, who had become the owner of Scott's bookmaking business, should have had the last word.

"To say that Archie Scott will be missed is obvious. To assess how much he will be missed is impossible. What can be said with certainty is that bookmakers everywhere owe him a debt of gratitude, and the good things he did on their behalf will live long after him. It might even be true to say that had Archie not lived, there might now be no bookmakers, for without him to plead our case, we might already have had a Tote Monopoly imposed upon us to the detriment of not only the bookmakers, but the whole racing public. I must have known Archie for more than thirty years, though I did not become closely associated with him until the early fifties when we did a great deal of association work together. He was at that time on the Board of the Southern BPA. The quality which impressed me most about Archie was his scrupulous fair-mindedness. He bent over backwards to be fair to everybody – except himself.

I had been nagging at him for years to give up some of the vast amount of his committee work, but this he refused to do until he was forced by his doctor to take it easy eighteen months ago. By then it was too late.

Not only was he completely fair-minded but he was able, through his example and personality, to instil others with a sense of fairness. We have this to thank him for, but, above all, we thank God that Archie Scott lived and worked among us."

Three months before the debate in the House of Lords, William had been interviewed by the BBC. He had taken a very unfavourable view of the report of the Royal Commission, in particular their advocacy of betting shops, towards which he had always been bitterly hostile.

In the BBC programme, *At Home And Abroad*, broadcast on March 23, 1956, Hill made it very clear that his views on betting shops had not changed.

Introducing the programme, Mr. Paul Leach of the BBC, said: "With the opening of a new Flat racing season, this would be one of the busiest weeks of the year if we had betting shops, following the recommendations of the Royal Commission on Betting and Lotteries. It is a controversial subject and we are now joined by leading bookmaker, Mr. William Hill.

Leach: Well, Mr. Hill, I suppose you agree with these proposals.

Hill: No, I certainly do not. I think it is a step in the wrong direction. I hope betting shops do not come into being, but if they do they will have to be strictly regulated.

Leach: Do you think the present law is ideal?

Hill: I think the present laws are chaotic and unfair because you cannot have a ready-money bet with a bookmaker through the post. You cannot legally have a bet with a street bookmaker, but you can send money with a Pools coupon, but not with a Racing coupon. It is ridiculous.

Leach: You think the proposal to set up betting shops is a bad idea?

Hill: I think it's a very bad idea, as I don't think it is necessary. We have got to have a change in the law, but why is it necessary to have betting shops? It will be quite sufficient if the law is changed to permit sending stakes through the post to a bookmaker and have a legal bet on the street. All that is necessary is that the bookmaker is licensed and that they have runners to take the bets back to the office, as they do now.

Leach: You would be in favour of the existing state of street betting being legalised, plus betting through the post. Don't you think there would be more social evils created, more street betting and, therefore, more loitering?

Hill: Certainly not. If betting shops were allowed I can visualise crowds of people inside and out during racing hours, and I don't think it would be very nice to see at every street corner, a betting shop with all these people hanging about.

Leach: They did not have these fears when opening betting shops in Ireland.

Hill: I have seen many betting shops, and I have seen these unpleasant types hanging about. I believe there is some law against crowding inside, but there is no law about crowding outside.

Leach: You think there must be some form of control if there are to be betting shops?

Hill: If they amend the law to have betting shops, and I sincerely hope they will not, there will have to be some proper authority to approve the premises. You cannot have 'hole-in-the-corner' dens. Most important of all, they will have to have proper hours allocated like public houses, and all betting shops must close during racing hours.

Leach: That is what the Royal Commission propose. Strict licensing of the premises and control of the way the premises are conducted. If you, Mr. Hill, don't think betting shops necessary, do you think it would be sufficient to repeal the present law and just have street betting by itself?

Hill: Will betting shops prevent street betting? Is everybody going to patronise shops where all those unpleasant types are hanging about?

Leach: Without going into the question of whether betting is morally wrong, while accepting that the present law is bad, we have got to do something. Do you think that Government control is the best alternative:

Hill: If they have control, the first thing they will have to do is to see that these shops are closed during racing hours.

As we all know now, the direct opposite of William's ideas and opinions have come about. TV is now on view at most betting shops, and these now command about 90 per cent of the total betting turnover.

11

One of William's failings was that he constantly under-rated the intelligence of his listeners, and his interview with Mr. Leach of the BBC evoked considerable merriment. For William Hill to moralise on the iniquities of those who would patronise betting shops was the joke of the year to those who did not know him.

Did William really think that listeners who knew anything about racing and bookmaking would believe that the reason for his opposition to betting shops was that 'he didn't think it would be very nice to see a betting shop at every street corner, with all those unpleasant types hanging about.' On the next occasion he attended a race meeting, he was greeted with a chorus of 'come off it, Bill, who do you think you're kidding?'

William's reply to the cynics was that he was also concerned that with a betting shop installed within a stone's throw of their homes, those in the lower income groups would be unable to resist the temptation to try to augment their weekly wages. They would lose and he visualised that these 'diabolical' shops, as he called them, would be responsible for a vast amount of misery and, in some cases, broken homes.

I am not suggesting that William's concern was not genuine, but why in the world did he not allude to this in his interview at the BBC, instead of confining himself to a dissertation on the undesirable types which would frequent these shops?

For as long as anyone could remember, the working man and his wife had always been able to get their shillings on, and the fact that it was against the law added to the fun – forbidden fruit always being the sweetest. I will not vouch for these figures, but I was reliably informed that prior to the licensing of betting shops, 75 per cent of the milkmen in working-class neighbourhoods acted as runners for bookmakers. A betting shop at the corner of the street would be a convenience, but it would not necessarily increase the size of a man's bet.

The cynics, largely composed of his fellow bookmakers, believed that William opposed the licensing of betting shops for one reason and one reason only, in that he realised their presence would be to the detriment of his own business. At that time, the firm of William Hill reigned almost supreme, both on the racecourse and in the starting price business; but if licences were granted to betting shops, anyone with sufficient capital and the enterprise to snatch the most propitious premises, would constitute a very serious rival to the Hill Organisation.

William foresaw that betting shops would completely transform betting in this country. The volume of the starting price and racecourse betting would inevitably dwindle, and he would have to reorganise his business from scratch. It was only natural that William should be perturbed by this prospect, and his thousands of well-satisfied clients would have sympathised with him had he not pretended that his opposition to the new form of betting was based on moral grounds.

Had street betting been legalised, the money would have been invested in his SP office by runners as it had always been, only in far greater quantities, while the sanction of postal betting would have resulted in thousands of letters all containing stake money, arriving at the Hill Organisation. With a betting shop at the corner of the street, no one in their right mind would send money by post to William Hill.

Rival firms such as Ladbrokes, Corals and Mecca almost immediately decided to take advantage of the new legislation, but William remained obstinately aloof, and a few years elapsed before he came off his high horse, and was persuaded by Bill Balshaw and others that if you can't beat them you must join them. A stormy interview between William and Bill Balshaw terminated with Balshaw exclaiming: "It's either betting shops or we go bust." For possibly the only time in his life William had to capitulate.

Every member of his executive staff knew that he was on the point of committing financial suicide, but William was the guv'nor and there was nothing they could do about it. It was said of the great jockey Steve Donoghue that he would have died a millionaire had he never got off a horse's back. William died a millionaire, but he would have been a multi-millionaire if he had never stepped down from that box on the rails which separates Tattersalls' ring from the members' enclosure and had left policy decisions to his very able business executives.

The greatest racecourse bookmaker who ever lived, William had an obstinate streak which more than once came near to bringing about his downfall. For a firm to give its rivals a three year start, thereby having to pay sky-high prices for suitable premises, and not only survive, but rise to greater heights than ever before, is a tribute to the name of William Hill and the skill and determination of those who served him.

The Peppiatt Committee was set up by the Government, under the chairmanship of Sir Leslie Peppiatt, to consider a levy on bookmakers which resulted in the Betting Levy Act of 1961. One outstanding difficulty facing this Committee was the thorny problem of how bookmakers should be assessed.

Lionel Barber, realising how unwilling bookmakers were to disclose their turnover on profits, suggested the system of categories, which was largely embodied in the first levy schemes. A vital flaw in the legislation was that the Bookmakers' Associations were not empowered to vet the applicants' permits, this vital job being left to the local magistrates, who, in all probability, knew nothing about racing, bookmakers, or the character of the men concerned. Some of their decisions were disastrous.

It is impossible to believe that those responsible for the Betting and Gaming Act foresaw such a bewildering extension of gambling as took place within the next five years. Betting shops were envisaged, but not the clubs and casinos, where the scale of play rivals Monte Carlo and Deavuille, not to mention the establishment of bingo as a national sport.

William told the Press that basically he agreed with the report of the Peppiatt Committee, in that it represented the desire of the bookmaking profession to make a contribution to racing. Little did he realise at the time that within four years the Levy Board would be demanding 12½ per cent of his profits. Hill told the journalists: "The money, already in excess of £1,000,000, should not go directly into the pockets of racecourse companies, but should be spent on providing additional amenities and reducing entrance fees".

He went on to say, 'I particularly want to see race-going made available to the working man on terms he can afford. To talk in sums of £3,000,000 (it was to be £8m in another three years) is kite-flying, and should be regarded as such until we find out what practical use is being made of the initial amount suggested by the Peppiatt Committee of £1¼m. I would strongly deprecate giving one penny piece to a racehorse owner or breeder, or the shareholders of racecourse companies. If they cannot survive without the subsidy, they should get out of the business".

Several months later, at a Press conference, William said. "I visualise the whole betting industry being nationalised, perhaps within five years. The tax of 25 per cent on Fixed Odds football betting levied by Mr. Maudling in his budget of 1964 deflecting, or so he must have hoped, all the wagers with Messrs. Hill, Ladbroke, Coral etc. into the hands of the Pools promoters was, in my view, the first move in this direction".

"I believe that the Government will quickly put into the shade the puny efforts of the Levy Board and the Turf authorities to gather money for the enrichment of owners, breeders and race-course shareholders. The Government will nationalise all the big bookmaking firms, all the betting shops, and instal their own agents for collecting purposes. All money would be channelled through the Totalisator and the Government would take 20 per cent of it without let or hindrance."

William reckoned that the Chancellor would be able to collect through the means of racing, football, greyhound racing and gambling clubs not less than £100 million a year. Then the Turf Board would have to go, cap in hand, to the Government and say please could they have a little money back for the purpose of continuing to run racing so that the Chancellor could collect more taxes.

In his April budget of 1964, Reginald Maudling succeeded in destroying the football empire that Hill had built up over the previous twenty-six years by imposing a 25 per cent tax on all Fixed Odds stakes.

William told the Press, "The Pool Promoters will be celebrating, and thanks to their lobbying, they will be drinking wine mixed with blood – bookmakers' blood. Fixed Odds are finished. In order to keep my staff, my plant and my offices occupied, it will be necessary for my firm to enter the Pools Field. Only when we cannot lose will we be happy to pay 25 per cent duty. For that reason, we shall direct all our energy into building up a pool."

"I shall carry on the Fixed Odds business for a while to see if there is any hope, but I very much doubt whether we could manage to break level in a season."

Whatever the tax was intended to realise, it raised in fact, barely £4½ million, of which William Hill (Football) Ltd. contributed £2½ million, according to *the Financial Times* of August 11, 1965. It is difficult to see why this tax was imposed against the advice of all those acquainted with the elementary principal of football betting, but William was in no doubt that it was the result of constant lobbying by the Pools Promoters and the politicians did as they were asked.

On June 29, 1965, Mr. Charles Layfield, in his address to the Annual General Meeting of the National Sporting League, declared that Mr. Maudling lost the General Election by imposing the ill-advised tax on Fixed Odds football. "He antagonised millions", said Mr. Layfield, "and killed an industry in three months". Mr. Layfield was absolutely right as hundreds of thousands of football fans bitterly resented being deprived of a little harmless amusement. The Hill Fixed Odds coupon, the first of its kind ever devised on a national basis, was designed to give the punter an attractive prospect, and a fair chance of winning. It started in 1939, and rose from a turnover on the first week of £6 to the astonishing figure in 1963 of over £16,000,000 [£128,000,000]. By 1952, the turnover had risen to £3 million, mainly through the industry of Hill's collectors' agents. It was a year of importance to the Hill football empire as Harry Hodgson arrived at Hill House.

Hodgson had been in the pools business since 1934, and had been director of I.T.P. Pools, which, in 1951, was amalgamated with Cope's. During the twelve years from 1952 until Budget Day, 1964, the Hill business expanded out of all recognition. There were several payouts of over a million pounds. The record in 1962 when the liability was over £1,300,000. Several individual winners of over £20,000 were paid out and, in 1964, the last year of the Fixed Odds coupon, there was a record win of £100,000 for £1. When one considers that this was an individual bet as opposed to a Pool investment, the return is colossal. Another week, over 200,000 punters were paid out and it was all completed by the Tuesday evening following the matches.

When betting shops were legalised in 1960, all shop proprietors who had an account with Hills became collecting agents for the company. All were entitled to distribute Fixed Odds coupons over the counter to their clients. A figure of £150,000 a week was normal, rising in mid-season to £400,000 a week, and on one occasion a total of £420,000 was reached. This was a fantastic sum of money to be betted on the happenings of one afternoon with one company and showed the national scale of interest in the Fixed Odds business which was destroyed by Mr. Maudling, while his successor, Mr. Callaghan, who was in full possession of the disastrous nature of the tax when he assumed office, increased the tax to 33 per cent. If ever there was a case of killing the goose that lays the golden egg, that was it.

William's decision to switch to Pools was thus described by the Financial Times: "Hill's decision follows the termination of the company's Fixed Odds betting service. The imposition of a 25 per cent tax on turnover, Hill claimed, resulted in a loss of £2.2 million last season after a provision of £2.57 million in duty."

The paper went on to say that the 2s. 0d. ordinary shares in Holders' Investment Trust fell to 6s. 6d. on the London Stock Exchange, following Mr. Callaghan's budget decision to retain the Fixed Odds duty. In Harry Hodgson's opinion, this was a political decision, as with the imposition of crippling new taxes such as Corporation Tax and Capital Gains Tax and with increased Income Tax, it was impossible to rescind any tax on gambling, even though the law of diminishing returns had rendered the tax completely obsolete.

The campaign for launching the first Hill Pools coupon was opened at a Press reception with William in the Chair on July 20, 1965. After remarking that all he wanted was a bit of peace and quiet in the last few years of his life, he said he was embarking on this perilous enterprise solely to give work to his staff. There was a complete absence of false optimism: "We are looking forward to the coming season with more hope than expectancy," William said. He thought that 95 per cent of their turnover in previous years came from clients who would not be interested in Pools betting. "This means", he continued, "that we must start all over again after taking twenty-five years to build up a Fixed Odds industry. William denied that he would seek or even accept a place among the Pools Promoters' Association, which comprises Littlewoods, Vernons, Cope's, Empire, Soccer and Zetters.

It was ironic that in the final months of Fixed Odds betting Hills should have achieved the world record payout of £100,000 for £1 for forecasting nine draws. The winner was Mr. Arthur Wyles, a British Rail welding inspector from Nottingham, who handed in his coupon over the counter of a local betting shop. When handing Mr. Wyles his cheque, William remarked that he hoped Mr. Wyles's success would not induce more people to patronise Hills Fixed Odds, adding: "The more money we take, the more we lose."

The results of the first three months, following the switch over to pool, were discouraging, to say the least. By the end of November, 1965, the turnover was only £60,000 a week and William knew that he needed at least £100,000 a week to break even. Most of his clientele of Fixed Odds backers, who knew about football and the value of prices, had disappeared and everything William had told Customs and Excise, when the Fixed Odds tax had been imposed, had come about.

Nevertheless, the disclosure on November 11, 1965 that Holders' Investment Trust had lost over £2½ million in the twelve months ending July 31, 1965, came as a shock to Stock Market operators. There was no dividend for shareholders as against one of 25 per cent in the previous year, when the profits had been £1¼ million. The loss, stated Lionel Barber, was due entirely to the payment of £2,572,000 in Fixed Odds betting duty.

The William Hill (Football) Ltd. story took another sensational turn when, in the first month of 1966, William announced he was about to re-enter the Fixed Odds field.

The next day, *The Sporting Life* said: "The news that William Hill Ltd. are to re-enter the Fixed Odds field is surprising to say the least of it. They were foremost in condemning the 25 per cent tax, as they said that it made such betting impossible. But unless they resign themselves permanently to the role of public benefactors, one must conclude that they have found that a 25 per cent tax is NOT impossible, all of which will bring joy to the Chancellor as he mulls over plans for an all round betting tax to the despair of all punters. The company will continue in the pools business as well as producing the new Fixed Odds coupon."

Pat Reekie, then P.R.O. to the Hills Organisation, replied to this article as follows:

"It is not unusual in the bookmaking profession for William Hill to be blamed for everything, though he has done more for his fellow bookmakers than any man living. *The Sporting Life* attacks him for going back into the Fixed Odds business, but why has *The Sporting Life* not attacked other pools firms who also run Fixed Odds coupons and have been doing so since the beginning of the season. It is precisely because of these other Fixed Odds coupons that Hills have now to provide a similar service for their clients. Many of our racing clients want a Fixed Odds bet, and the trade want to be able to hedge on football."

The Editor of *The Sporting Life* replied:

"The sad fact is that the last bastion has fallen: Hills, the former leaders in Fixed Odds betting, and most outspoken critic of the tax, have abandoned what was a courageous stand. That they should have been forced to do so as a result of the customary dis-unity of bookmakers and their regrettable propensity for putting immediate gain before the long-term interests of their profession, is beside the point at issue."

The Editor of *The Sporting Life* had hit the nail on the head. While cynics in the world of commerce maintain that the Eleventh Commandment – 'Thou shalt not be found out' – is the most important. Bookmakers, who for the most part have little to hide, have substituted: 'Thou shalt not love they neighbour – if he happens to be another bookmaker.'

A letter from a West Country bookmaker provides a good example of disunity between bookmakers and their disinclination to unite in the face of common foe:

"Hills are a fine firm but I am getting a bit sick of the image of Mr. William Hill the Great Leader, as portrayed mainly by his employees. Whichever way you look at it, Hills have made themselves look very foolish over Fixed Odds football. I do not think there would ever have been a tax if Hills had not created the basis for its easy collection by offering over the odds and putting the small man throughout the country out of business.

This had the effect of putting a very large part of the Fixed Odds betting into the hands of one firm. In turn, this led to the most idiotic and undignified war between Hills and Ladbrokes, and, most important, to their invasion of the Pools area of operation, with betting on what was virtually the treble chance. The Pools, with their high tax, were thus operating at a serious disadvantage. So who could blame them for lobbying for either no tax at all, or a tax on Fixed Odds as well as on the Pools? The traditional form of Fixed Odds betting is as different from pools betting as chalk from cheese, but Hills and Ladbrokes changed all that and paid the penalty.

Once the tax was on, it was plain that the bonanza was over, and it only now remained either to bet at realistic odds or pack up. But Hills and Ladbrokes did neither, they went on down the dizzy slope towards financial disaster and inevitably got badly mauled. When Hills were forced to finish Fixed Odds betting, high-principled statements were made that they would never again operate a Fixed Odds coupon until the iniquitous tax was removed, which is why they now appear so silly, particularly following the lack of success of Hills' entry into the Pools business.

Personally, I cannot understand what Mr. Hill has done for bookmaking that is so wonderful. Perhaps I am only an ill-informed provincial, but the way I see it, bookmaking has done a hell of a lot for Mr. Hill.

He is a clever business man, and is entitled to have made his pile, but I do not think he is doing anyone in the book-making business a favour when he appears on television and tells people not to bet, but if they must bet to do so with Hills.

Again, he has been an implacable enemy of betting shops, which, surely, are the results of legislation in favour of the working man. Perhaps, as a result of his great success in the credit field, he has advanced so far into the upper strata that he regards betting shops as vulgar, and thinks it better that the lower classes should continue to have their bob furtively and illegally with the milkman, rather than have the facilities that have always been available to their social superiors. It is also, of course, obvious that betting shops must pinch business from Hill's credit set up. The contention that Hill is not liable to be criticised like the rest of us, is completely ridiculous. Let us have no more eulogies and no more declarations from Olympus.

H. P. Hooper, Managing Director, Hooper's of Plymouth (Cash Betting) Ltd."

This letter aroused a critical eulogy from someone who signed himself 'Ex-employee':

"The attitude of many bookmakers towards William Hill's achievements is akin to that of eunuchs towards sex: if you can't do it, knock it. As one who has been in a better position than most to evaluate William Hill, I stand by my view that Hill has done more to improve the bookmakers' image than any other man in the business. Of course he has made mistakes, but if Hill, by his mistakes, added to his burdens he did not ask for any assistance from Mr. Hooper, or anyone else in the bookmaking business, in carrying them.

With a colossal turnover at Hill House, and his mastery of betting, Hill could have manipulated the starting price market. But far from doing this for his own ends, the only valid criticism that could be levelled at Hill is that his decision to stand his ground has diverted the flow of money from the course. But you can't blame Hill for that. The cause is the greed of the bookmakers who would rather take commission from Hill, than earn money on the racecourse. If Hill is no longer a force in bookmaking politics, it is because he has chosen not to take the reins which would be easily thrust into his hands should he feel the desire to crack the whip.

The rock of Gibraltar may have outlived its usefulness, but it still remains a symbol of British tradition, and like the rock, you cannot write William Hill off in two columns of *The Sporting Life*. If Mr. Hooper and his colleagues goad William Hill still further, they may cause him to recant his views on betting shops, and if the name William Hill goes up on a betting shop next to yours, you may as well shut up shop."

By the time of William's death in October, 1971, the football business had been discontinued, and the able Harry Hodgson's attentions were fully occupied with running the betting shops. The wheel had gone full circle. What had started twenty-five years ago as an adjunct to the racing business, mainly to keep the staff busy during the winter months, had within twelve years outgrown the racing end five-fold. Now racing again predominates, and as William was a racing man and always had been, perhaps this was for the best.

His venture into Pools did not last long and in August, 1966, the closure was applied and for the 1966–67 season William announced that despite the 25 per cent tax, only a fixed odds coupon would be sent out.

12

Few men have had a more profound impact on modern racing than Phil Bull. Richard Baerlein stated in *The Observer* that he was the most influential figure in British racing during the post-war years. Baerlein went on to say that Bull's publications present us every week with a wealth of information and that he has put the appraisal of the merits of racehorses on a new footing, intelligible to everyone. There is no doubt that Phil Bull had done more than anyone to educate the racing public and improve their chances of getting the better of the bookmakers.

Over the years, Bull made a great deal of money backing horses, though he had his lean times. His breeding successes were considerable, though he never bred a classic winner. Probably the best horse he bred was Romulus who, although he failed to win the Two Thousand Guineas in 1962, went on to prove himself the best miler in Europe. William Hill and Phil Bull were friends for over twenty-five years. William had been perplexed by a number of winning accounts which, normally, would not have shown a profit. He made some enquiries and found that these punters were following a system devised by William K. Temple, B.Sc. One day his telephone rang and a voice announced itself as Mr. Bull, someone William had never heard of. Bull accused William Hill of advertising under false pretences, adding: "You advertise daily that you have 'No Limit' terms and yet I understand that some of your clients are not allowed to bet at 'Tote odds.'" "What's it got to do with you?" William asked. "Are you one of Temple's clients?" "I am William K. Temple", said Bull.

Bull's recollection of their first conversation is different. According to him, one or two of the clients of W. K. Temple had had their accounts closed by Hill so he rang William and protested, saying that the bookmaker should be prepared to pay winning punters as well as losers. At that time, Bull was a school teacher in South London and was running the *Temple Time Test* only as a secondary occupation. He was anxious to get out of the teaching profession, and after his conversation with William went to work in his offices in Park Lane.

Generally speaking, although they had their differences, the racecourse partnership between William Hill and Phil Bull was very much to their mutual advantage. Bull's advice on the prospects of the various horses was not always accepted, although William recognised Bull's views as being based on a scientific study of time, going, weather conditions, etc., factors which had seldom been taken into account prior to Bull's arrival on the Turf.

In 1941, Bull became a winning owner for the first time. He saw a filly in the paddock at Newmarket which really attracted him. He thought she was the most marvellous walker he had ever seen and a charming filly in every way. She was the Eclair filly (in 1941 two-year-olds were permitted to run un-named). Bull recalls that on going to the sales at Newmarket the following year, he opened his catalogue and saw the name of the filly he had admired so much. He had been doing pretty well backing horses and had about £2,500 in the bank. It was war time, prices were low and he thought he would be able to buy her for £2,500, which was all he had in the world. But others had also admired this filly and Bull had to go to £3,500 [£60,000] to buy her.

Immediately the sale was concluded, Bull rang William. He told him he had bought a horse, could not raise the total purchase money and would William lend him a £1,000 [£17,000]. William told Bull that he was not quite right in the head, but he nevertheless loaned him the £1,000. Bull named the filly Lady Electra and she won him ten races, including the substitute Lincolnshire Handicap.

At stud she was not a great success but she bred Queen Electra (by Big Game), who staked herself as a yearling and never raced, but she was the dam of Eudaemon, who won the Gimcrack Stakes at York in 1956.

Bull tried very hard to persuade William to buy Dante, by Nearco out of Rosy Legend when he came up as a yearling at the Newmarket Sales. For some reason William was not very enthusiastic and Dante, the property of Sir Eric Ohlson, did not fetch his reserve.

From the moment that Dante won his first race as a two-year-old at Stockton, it was obvious that William had missed out on a good thing. Bull thought that Sir Eric might still be prepared to sell Dante for £10,000 [£170,000] but William offered only £7,000 [£119,000] and his offer was turned down. When Dante won the Derby, Bull had the biggest win of his life up until then. The day following the Derby, William, Bull and some members of the Crazy Gang drove back to London – Bull and Hill in one car and Bud Flanagan and the Crazy Gang in another. As they pulled up on the road to have a drink, Bud Flanagan and his party got out of their car and knelt down on the grass verge to pay homage to Bull because he had made them all have a big bet on Dante.

When William bought Whitsbury Manor towards the end of the war, Bull went down with him to inspect the place which William bought for about £60,000 [£1,020,000]. Bull admits that at the time it was a curious choice for a stud, situated as it was on the edge of the New Forest. It did not occur to him then that it would become almost the most successful stud in the country.

Bull was entirely responsible for William buying the mare Kong, at the bargain price of £750. I have already described how her son Nimbus, by Nearco, won the Derby, she was also the dam of Grey Sovereign, a brilliantly fast racehorse and an even more successful stallion. Grey Sovereign was by Nearco's son Nasrullah. Bull described the purchase of Kong, one of the greatest bargains in the history of the Turf, as 'just a bit of luck.'

In the early fifties, Bull went to live in the North and ceased to work for Hill's offices. Captain C. R. (Peter) Parsons then took over the management of Hill's studs and breeding interests. After Bull's move north he became William's racing manager. In the mid-fifties, William complained to Bull that whereas the horses Bull was breeding and racing were having considerable success, his own horses were not. Bull thought that perhaps William's horses were not properly placed, adding that his horses were not better bred than William's but were winning races because they were. At Bull's suggestion William sent his horses to Malton to be managed by Bull and trained by Captain Charles Elsey.

In 1958 one of these included a filly called Cantelo, by Chanteur II – Rustic Bridge. She was un-defeated in five races as a two-year-old, but it was not until her last race in the Royal Lodge Stakes at Ascot that Bull realised that she was a classic filly in the making. She was a terror at the gate, and it was only the patience of the starter Alec Marsh which prevented her being left at the post. She won decisively and Bull now realised she was a bloody good filly.

In 1960 her first race as a three-year-old was in the Cheshire

Oaks at Chester which she won in great style. She was then put by for the Oaks at Epsom, but it was her misfortune to be foaled in the same year as the Aly Khan's Petite Etoile, one of the most brilliant fillies of all time. It was Cantelo's further misfortune that the going was very firm indeed. She went on to win the Ribblesdale Stakes at Royal Ascot, and the following month finished fourth to Alcide (one of the best post-war colts), in the King George VI and Queen Elizabeth Stakes before going to Doncaster in September.

The St. Leger was run on Saturday, and on the Wednesday Cantelo ran in the Park Hill Stakes, one of the most important races for fillies. On all form, William Hill's filly looked a certainty and odds of 9–4 were freely laid on her. Bull does not think that Edward Hide rode one of his best races on William's hot favourite. Having taken the lead soon after entering the straight, Hide looked round and realised he had Mirnaya and Discorea, whom he had regarded as Cantelo's principal opponents, were beaten, so he did not push her out.

He had not reckoned with Collyria, the horse Lester Piggott had chosen to ride in the One Thousand Guineas in preference to Petite Etoile. Although Collyria had failed to show her true form as a three-year-old, Noel Murless had never been in any doubt that she was a high-class filly, and she came along with a great run to catch Cantelo in the final furlong and win at 33–1. Cantelo was none the worse for the race, rather the reverse, and after due consideration Bull and William decided to run her in the St. Leger three days later, although they did not think that she had much chance of winning. I do not think I can do better than quote from Phil Bull's book, *Racehorses Of 1959*, to describe what happened on that memorable occasion at Doncaster.

"Not since Apology's Victory had a horse trained in Yorkshire won a St. Leger, but the reception accorded Cantelo was vastly different from that given to the winner of 1874, when one chronicler reported that never before had such a demonstration of enthusiasm been witnessed at Doncaster. The heroine of the hour was met by an enthusiastic crowd who cheered again and again as the filly was led to the door of the weighing room.

He goes on to say: "Perhaps it is unfair to assume that the enthusiasts in 1874 had backed the winner, but it is certain that those who gave vent to their spleen in 1959 had not, and if it cannot be said, as was reported after Thormanby's St. Leger defeat that Cantelo's victory was greeted by a perfect yell of fury.

It was received with a marked absence of enthusiasm, and a certain amount of vocal disapproval. The reason for the unfavourable reception of Cantelo was the discrepancy between her running in the Park Hill Stakes and in the St. Leger. Cantelo's victory cannot be described as other than surprising, and on the racecourse there are always those who take the line that the unexpected is the consequence of sharp practice. This view is all the more readily supported when the owner of the horse in question is a bookmaker."

Hide had not set out with the intention of giving Cantelo an easy race in the Park Hill Stakes, although in view of previous form he was justified in thinking that he could win the race without being unduly severe on his mount. The race was run at a slow pace early on, and Bull maintained that the correct tactics would have been for Hide to send Cantelo about her business from the entry into the straight.

Cantelo had been handicapped in top class races by her lack of a turn of foot. As the St. Leger was run at a fast pace throughout, the premium was on stamina, which was all to Cantelo's advantage, but it was difficult to understand how anyone could have seriously envisaged her winning the race on firm ground, whatever the result of the Park Hill Stakes had been. In the King George VI and Queen Elizabeth Stakes, Cantelo had shown herself to be 12lb inferior to Alcide at weight for age, which could not entitle her to be fancied to beat the Derby winner Parthia, though it must be remembered that Alcide had won the previous year's St. Leger by eight lengths.

Cantelo needed plenty of work and her trainer believed that she was short of a gallop when she ran for the first time at Doncaster. That race brought her to concert pitch and Cantelo was never out of the first three. She took the lead three furlongs from home and beat Fidalgo, second in the Derby, by a length-and-a-half.

The vocal demonstration as Cantelo stood in the unsaddling enclosure was ridiculous. William did not have a shilling on her and had not backed one of his horses for many years. But all the racegoers could see was that a horse owned by a bookmaker, William Hill, had been beaten at 9–4 and won the St. Leger at 100–7 three days later.

Bull managed William's horses in the North for nine years and during that time, everything he had promised was borne out. Bull recalled that only two of William's horses, which were managed by him failed to win a race. Basically, however, William was no longer an owner, he was a breeder and a successful breeder at that. He was an owner only in so far as he wished to retain fillies which he had bred to go to the stud and he wanted to win races with them before they did. His main concern was to breed good horses and sell them at public auction, and only those which failed to make their reserve were put into training.

It stands to reason that having known William for more than twenty-five years, Bull had some very decided views as to his character and temperament. Although some people considered William 'tight' where money was concerned, Bull is of the opinion that the reverse was true. As soon as a man is described as a millionaire, everybody treats him as fair game. It did not take William very long to realise this, and not only was he careful in small matters, he scrutinised each and every bill he received and more often than not queried it. William's character is illustrated by his action with regard to the family of an employee who had robbed him of a large sum of money. William was very angry but although he sacked the man and was forced to prosecute him, he supported the man's wife and her two children while he was in prison, and when they were old enough to go away to school, paid for their education. Although it was not apparent to the casual observer, William was much concerned for other people and had a highly developed social conscience. What he did not have was the capacity to translate this into his relationships with individuals. I have already referred to his inability to pat a man on the back and say 'well done', not because he did not realise that the man had done a good job, but because he had some mental block which prevented him from expressing admiration. Bull said: "I know I did a great number of things that pleased him, but he never once told me so, and that's what gets people down."

88

Hill was far from incapable of telling a man when he had done something wrong, and did not mince his words. Bull thought that this came from his early days in Birmingham when he had to struggle for his existence by self-assertion. It was bred into his character and remained with him throughout his life.

Although William had the most fantastic memory for faces and figures, both human and mathematically, his recollection of facts and events was very sketchy. The tape recordings made by him in the last years of his life are full of errors. One of the most glaring of these was his assertion that Pearl Diver, the winner of the 1947 Derby, was owned by M. Magot and trained by Henry Count. Everyone interested in racing knows that Pearl Diver was owned by Baron Geoffrey De Waldner, trained by Percy Carter in France, and sent for his final preparation to Claude Halsey at Newmarket. No one should have had a better recollection than William of Pearl Diver's victory or perhaps, the defeat of Tudor Minstrel, as this was easily the most decisive factor in William's climb to the top.

After his retirement, William got into the habit of sitting back in his armchair with his thumbs in his braces, holding forth to those prepared to listen to him. His audience often included Quintin Gilbey's brother Geoffrey, who knew William better than he did, and had a great affection for him. Geoffrey never forgot the details of a race run over the previous sixty years, although he sometimes forgot a name, and William's accuracies when reminiscing never ceased to surprise him. William, of course, would never admit he was wrong, so it was pointless to question the accuracy of his statements.

I have described William's political views, and the reasons he gave me for them which conflicted with those of most capitalists – and William was indeed a capitalist. His religious views were those of an agnostic. Phil Bull, on the other hand, was the most convinced atheist I have ever met. Any suggestion of the existence of God will evoke a plea to, "Get rid of this mythology". William was never at a loss for words, but he was fairly inarticulate and incapable of making a convincing case on any subject off the cuff however near to his heart, or pocket, it may have been. Phil Bull however, had an agile mind and an excellent command of the English language and could argue, successfully, that black was white!

In what Quintin says was the most articulate letter he ever received, written in 1970, Phil Bull wrote:

"You'll be dead soon. So will I. Do you really think there's some survival for you somewhere? Where? In what form? Up in the skies as a spirit? You know the extent of the Universe: that light takes 10,000 million years to cross our own galaxy, and that there are thousands of millions of such galaxies. Let's face it, you and I are insignificant little pieces of living matter on a minor planet."

I am quite sure that Phil Bull put forward similar arguments to William, but apparently without convincing him, as although he did not attend church services, he made generous donations to Whitsbury Parish Church. William had one characteristic in common with Miss Dorothy Paget – he was determined to hide his light under a bushel, where philanthropy was concerned. He gave liberally to those in need, but went to great lengths to conceal his altruism from the outside world.

13

William Hill's rise to the top of the breeding industry was nearly as spectacular as the manner in which he rose from obscurity to Britain's leading bookmaker in the space of ten years. By 1961, less than twenty years after he acquired the Whitsbury and Sezincote studs, which were amalgamated the same year as William Hill Studs Ltd., his success was so phenomenal that he invariably finished in the first four or five in the list of breeders, a feat which had taken other famous studs more than fifty years to achieve. The batch of eighteen yearlings submitted by William at the new October sales in 1965 netted an all time record, for a single vendor, of some 124,650 gns. [£1,000,000].

Sezincote, the smaller of the two properties, was built and owned by the late Mr. J. A. Hirst, a retired electrical engineer. Hirst went about his business in a most thorough manner, carrying out investigations as to the most suitable soil available for stud purposes. His conclusions led him to the Cotswolds, where he leased forty acres on the east side of the road between Broadway and Stow-on-the-Wold. He erected the most lavish set of stud buildings, comprising six splendid boxes, together with a saddle room and stud grooms' cottage, all in Cotswold stone. When Mr. Hirst died in 1945, William purchased the majority of the shares from the executors, one of whom was the late Mr. J. A. Weir Johnston. This gentleman was something of an eccentric in that he disliked prose and conducted most of his business in verse.

By 1951, William owned the stud outright, and had added to it considerably. Sezincote now is a stud of 300 acres, of which sixty are farm. Mr. 'Peter' Parsons was the stud manager until his retirement in 1963. His successor was the resident manager, Mr. Norman Lonsdale.

Home is where the heart is and there is no doubt that William Hill's spiritual home was Whitsbury. Whitsbury is a long, narrow property stretching from the stud on one side to the end of the gallops on the other, a distance of about three miles. With the additions that have been made to it, it embraces some 2,000 acres, 170 of which make up the private and public stud.

Shortly after he had purchased Whitsbury, William installed

'Monty' Smyth as public trainer at the Whitsbury stables, previously occupied by Norman Scobie who trained for Sir Charles Hyde, the previous owner of Whitsbury. Subsequently, Sir Gordon Richards became William's tenant and a public trainer, and remained such until his retirement. The two men got on reasonably well, although I can well remember each of them telling me what a hard bargain the other could strike.

On the retirement of Sir Gordon Richards, Bill Marshall moved into the Whitsbury stables, where he enjoyed great success. William, in his later years, was not interested in the racing side of Whitsbury. All his attention was centred on his herd of friesians, which produced more than 100,000 gallons of milk a year and the stud, which is divided into two separate parts; one for visiting mares, and the other for William's mares and stallions and their offspring.

The first Whitsbury yearlings which William sent up to the 1947 Newmarket sales included two colts by Nearco. The one out of Kong was Nimbus. I have already described how he was sold to Mr. Glenister for 5,000 gns, as a birthday present to his wife. The other, out of Sol d'Or was named Jai Hind. He was sold to the Gaekwar of Baroda for 10,000 gns. The following year Kong's son by Nearula fetched 6,700 gns. and was a tremendous bargain. Grey Sovereign was his name, and he won £8,000 on the racecourse, but it was as a stallion that he was so fabulously successful. Up until the end of 1965, he had sired the winners of over 350 races worth £271,000, and in the same period 120 yearlings which were sold for £364,000, (worth several million nowadays).

In the summer of 1949 Kong was killed in her paddock, she was in her prime. She was found in the paddock with a fractured skull, presumably having been kicked by another mare. The tragedy was heightened by the fact that the post-mortem revealed she was carrying a filly foal by Big Game, who would have been worth a King's ransom. An absolute tragedy.

Between 1946 and the time of Kong's death, William began to increase his number of brood mares, the most successful of which was Vertencia. Bred in France, she won two races for him, including the Park Hill Stakes at Doncaster. I have described how she was beaten by a matter of six inches in the 1948 Cesarewitch when William had backed her to win him £33,000. In her first season at stud, Vertencia produced a chestnut filly by Chanteur II named Warning. Warning was bought by Mr. J. J. Astor for 7,200 gns. She was not much good on the racecourse but produced five winners in as many years at stud; including Escourt who finished fourth in the 1962 Derby.

The following year, Vertencia gave birth to a colt by Nearco called By Thunder, for which Mr. Jack Gerber paid 8,000 gns. By Thunder won the Ebor Handicap in 1954 and five other races.

In 1953, William decided to keep most of the fillies which his mares produced, a policy which paid off handsomely. He made an exception, however, in the case of Cretencia, a yearling filly by Crepello, for which the Duke of Norfolk paid 16,000 gns., the second highest price of the year.

The next major success for William was when he purchased a mare called Rustic Broom, by Bois Roussel, out of Wyn, who, though useless on the racecourse, made her name as a brood mare and produced a Classic winner by Chanteur II in Cantelo, who was her second foal. Considering that William bought Rustic Broom for only 4,600 gns., she must be regarded as one of his biggest bargains.

In 1953, William made one of his shrewdest purchases when he acquired the eight-year-old mare Fair Freedom for 3,000 gns. Bred by Miss Dorothy Paget, this un-raced mare had already bred two good winners, and proved an outstanding success at stud, producing fourteen foals in as many years. The best known of Fair Freedom's offspring were William's filly called Be Careful and Liberal Lady who, after winning five races for Mr. A. C. Walking, a retired baker, was sold to the USA, where she won more than $60,000.

Be Careful, by My Babu, was born in 1956, a year after Liberal Lady, and her success in the Gimcrack Stakes at York in 1958 gave William great satisfaction, after the victories of Nimbus and Cantelo. She was only a small filly when she won the Gimcrack, the Champagne Stakes at Doncaster and a race at Goodwood, netting her owner £11,000 [£143,000] as a two-year-old. William much appreciated the honour of giving the principal speech at the Annual dinner of the Gimcrack Club in York. He had plenty to say, not all of it acceptable to some of his highly placed listeners. He began by saying that he was the first bookmaker ever to win the Gimcrack.

"Betting is the life blood of the racing industry", he said. And continued: "I believe the future of horse-racing and British Bloodstock depends entirely on the patronage of the punters, the paying customers at the turnstiles. Whether it is a good thing or not, the majority of people go racing, not because of their love of horse flesh, nor because it is the Sport of Kings, but because they want to bet."

Although he did not refer to the matter in his Gimcrack speech, William felt that he was humiliated every time he wished to enter a Members' enclosure, in that he had to go to an office and be vetted by some teenage girl possibly with no knowledge of racing whatsoever. He had bred a Derby winner, and bred and owned a winner of a St. Leger, and had imported a great horse in Chanteur II and numerous high class stallions, thereby raising the standard of bloodstock in this country. But simply and solely because he was a bookmaker, he was regarded as an undesirable person.

It is a rule on every racecourse that no one shall make a book in the Members' enclosure, and if a bookmaker attempted to do so, he would quite rightly be ejected, but to debar a man from belonging to a club because he belonged to a certain profession, and an honourable profession at that, William considered unconstitutional. As number one bookmaker, it was appropriate that he should be first bookmaker to become a sponsor. The race was the Ebor Handicap in 1957, won by Morecambe. This was followed by the Redcar Gold Cup in 1959.

William had always had a very great regard for Major Leslie Petch, who was clerk of the course at both these meetings, and it was on account of this that his sponsorship activities started up in the north.

14

A young actor, with little knowledge of racing, once asked the great Tom Walls, who owned and trained the Derby winner April Fifth whether he fancied one of his horses which was due to run that afternoon. "I do not", snapped Tom, to which the young actor asked the great man whether he meant he was going to have it stopped. "Stopped?", roared Tom. "Don't be daft, he's like you – no bloody good, and he'll stop himself, like one of your cheques".

This anecdote leads up to the famous action for slander brought against William Hill by Norman Scobie, his trainer in January, 1947. The action arose from a dispute following the victory of a two-year-old colt called Vilmorin at Salisbury in 1945. Vilmorin had landed a most elaborately worked coup in which every device had been employed to throw dust in the eyes of both backers and bookmakers. So successful were these devices that Vilmorin, who subsequently became a highly successful sprinter and a prolific sire of sprinters, started at 25–1.

The ruse began by Scobie deciding to put up a minute jockey called Sharpe, although Vilmorin was due to carry 9st. The appearance of Sharpe's name on the number board was tantamount to telling the world that Vilmorin was not fancied. This nice little man, who was in his forties, had rarely been permitted to ride a fancied horse carrying more than 7st, and here he was riding one carrying 9st. Every punter and bookmaker made a mental note that Vilmorin was at least one horse they need not bother about. The illusion was carried still farther by Hill repeatedly offering 25–1 on Vilmorin. Needless to say, there were no takers.

When Sharpe was told that Vilmorin was fancied as he was being led out of the paddock onto the course, he could hardly believe his ears. The message had to be repeated to him as he sat spellbound, with the best part of 3st of dead weight between himself and his mount. Scobie had tried Vilmorin, barring accidents, to be a certainty, and all Sharpe had to do was to sit there and let Vilmorin do the rest.

Vilmorin was the property of Mr. John Read, a wealthy Wiltshire farmer and William was entrusted with a stable commission of £600 each way. After the race he reported that he had been able to place only £500 each way on Vilmorin. Even this sum netted a profit of over £15,000 [£255,000].

Mr. Read and Scobie took William before Tattersalls' Committee who rather surprisingly ruled in Hill's favour. William had agreed to put on £600 each way, and in the world of betting, a man's word is as good as his bond. But what had happened was that William had been able to get £500 on at starting price without disturbing the market, but he knew that if he tried to get a further £100 each way on Vilmorin, it might have 'blown the gaff' and the horse's price would have come tumbling down. This was no business of Tattersalls' Committee, although they thought it was.

There is no suggestion that William had acted dishonourably as £500 each way at 25–1 is a better proposition than £600 each way at 6–1. One would imagine that a man of Scobie's experience would have appreciated this and if he had that would have been the end of the matter.

For a man so much in the public eye, and with his vast and diverse business interests, William indulged in remarkably little litigation. The case of Norman Scobie versus William Hill, which was heard in the High Court on January 29, 1947 before Mr. Justice Croom-Johnston, was for slander. Scobie alleged that outside the committee room at Tattersalls' Hill had called him an 'imposter and an Australian bush-ranger'. Mr. G. O. Slade, K.C., and Mr. P. M. Morie appeared for Scobie, and Sir Patrick Hastings, K.C., and Mr. Gerald Gardiner (later Lord Gardiner, the Lord Chancellor) for William.

William denied using the words and pleaded alternatively that they were 'vulgar abuse' and that they were not actionable. Scobie had acted as private trainer at Whitsbury to the late Sir Charles Hyde, and on his death, when the property was acquired by William Hill (Park Lane) Ltd. he remained as trainer for William. Mr. Slade said: "I want to avoid saying anything which can possibly cast any aspersion on the company because bookmakers live by their good name, and I am not going to allow the fair name of the company to be in any way prejudiced by what has been a private dispute between Mr. Scobie and Mr. Hill."

The dispute concerning bets was in no way relevant to the

case, which was simply and solely one of alleged slander. Nevertheless, Mr. Slade said: "The decision of Tattersalls' Committee on the day the alleged slander was published was astonishing."

Sir Patrick Hastings protested: "As your Lordship knows, betting men put their disputes before a betting committee. It is not for this Court to say that this was an 'astonishing decision.'"

Mr. Slade replied: "Astonishing is a masterpiece of understatement."

Mr. Slade continued: "It was while Mr. Hill and Mr. Scobie were coming out of the committee room that Hill, in the presence of a score or more people waiting for cases to be heard, published the slander complained of."

As betting was not then recognised in this country, and bets are not recoverable by law, it is difficult to understand as to why Mr. Croome-Johnston allowed opposing counsels to indulge in long, drawn out arguments as to the correctness of Tattersalls' decision. Mr. Slade appeared to be getting the better of the argument when Sir Patrick Hastings asked: "Is your Lordship going to be asked whether Tattersalls' decision was right or wrong? If it is suggested it showed malice, I will admit that outside the Committee Room Mr. Scobie and Mr. Hill were abusing each other like pickpockets."

Mr. Slade went on to say that to call a man an imposter, and an Australian bush-ranger, constituted a serious allegation, which he must either withdraw or prove. Quoting dictionary definitions of the word 'bush-ranger', Mr. Slade said that in the Concise Oxford Dictionary it meant 'An Australian brigand, an escaped convict, living in the bush.' The word 'brigand' was defined as 'bandit, robber.'

Speaking as one who has watched a race at Tattenham Corner and heard what the jockeys call one another as they jostle in the Derby for a good position, it would seem to me that 'Australian bush-ranger' was a very mild form of opprobium.

Mr. Slade said he was not suggesting that Hill meant that Scobie was a bush-ranger, as Australian bush-rangers existed in the early 19th century, but that he was a thief and a robber. Letters were referred to between Scobie and Hill when it came to Scobie's knowledge that in September, 1945, William had contemplated sacking Scobie and appointing 'Monty Smyth' as trainer at Whitsbury. In one letter William had written, "I have tolerated your rude letters in the past – this is the last opportunity you will have of being disrespectful to me. As you propose to give notice, I give *you* notice on behalf of the company to terminate your engagement."

Scobie replied, "My letters to you did not reveal any impertinence unless plain speaking can be described as such."

Questioned about the alleged slander, Scobie said: "Hill called me an imposter and an Australian bush-ranger in the presence of a crowd of people all concerned with racing – bookmakers and their clients, and I told him that this was a very serious allegation you have made in front of these people and one which may endanger my livelihood. You must either withdraw it or prove it."

Sir Patrick: (cross-examining): What in the world have you brought this action for?

Scobie: I can't stand aside and let this man cast aspersions on my character.

Sir Patrick: What do you think the aspersions were? Did you ever meet a bush-ranger?

Scobie: No.

Sir Patrick: Did you ever meet anyone who has ever met a bush-ranger?

Scobie: Yes, I met an old policeman who fought against the Kelly gang.

Sir Patrick: When you and Mr. Hill came out of the Committee room were you both extremely angry?

Scobie: No, sir, I was disappointed.

Sir Patrick: Did you say to Mr. Hill, "I will make you sit up for this?"

Scobie: No, sir.

Sir Patrick: Did you say, "You have always liked publicity and I will bloody see you get it before I finish with you."

Scobie: No, sir.

Sir Patrick: Did Mr. Hill say, "You are nothing but a ponce?" And did he go on to say, "You have been poncing all your life, it's about time you went back to Australia where you belong?"

Scobie: He did not say these things.

Sir Patrick: You were both very angry, but was not Mr. Hill's observation a joking one?

Scobie: It was not joking.

Opening the case for the defence, Sir Patrick Hastings described the action as 'ridiculous.'

"Here is a case of two racing men who were very angry. I don't think either of them knows what happened. Somebody called somebody something, and out of it this monumental action has arisen. I consider it absurd that the Court's time should be occupied with such a case. If you were to take all this away from Tattersalls' and put it at the door of a public house, it would be exactly the same: angry men shouting at one another.

It is ridiculous to suggest that, as was pleaded as an innuendo, that Mr. Scobie was an 'escaped convict' who had taken to the bush in order to lead a predatory life."

William Hill, giving evidence, said that Scobie was in a raging temper as he emerged from the committee room, and was provoking him all along the passage. "I did call him a ponce, but I cannot remember calling him a bush-ranger."

Sir Patrick: What did you mean by ponce?
Hill: I tried to express my feelings in as strong a manner as possible. I meant he was a parasite and a sponger.
Sir Patrick: Did you ever mention the words "Australian bush-ranger"?
Hill: No, I don't know the meaning of the word.

Giving judgment, Mr. Justice Croom-Johnston said the case in all its essentials was one of the utmost simplicity. He did not propose to go into the details of the betting transactions between the parties, or to excite the greed and avarice of those who had listened through the evidence by stating the amount of the winnings. It was impossible for his Lordship to say that the plaintiff had satisfied him that the words of which he complained were spoken.

Judgment for the defendant with costs was entered. Norman Scobie lived until he was well into his nineties. All William's major court cases went in his favour, thanks to Sir Patrick Hastings, and later, Lord Gardiner.

15

It is not often given to ordinary mortals 'To See Ourselves As Others See Us', but the great ones have the dubious satisfaction of seeing (too often in some cases) how they are regarded by others. Articles in the national Press, and interviews on radio and television project the public, if not the private image, of the person in question.

For the last twenty-five years of his life, William was subjected (not unwillingly, as he liked to air his views on a variety of topics) to such treatment, and during the time of betting legislation between 1956 and 1961 he was repeatedly canvassed by all the purveyors of mass media. However, it is when the heat is not on, that the journalist or interviewer can get a more objective view, and a truer picture of the man emerges.

From an article in *The New Statesman*, by John Morgan, in April, 1964 under the heading 'The Biggest Bookie In The World', a picture emerges of William as a social thinker and philosopher, his private conscience perpetually at war with his business interests and intentions. Mr. Morgan wrote:

"The biggest gambling factory in history stands eight storeys high just across Blackfriars Bridge. In the expensively cooled basement an I.C.T. computer, costing £150,000, [£1,200,000] flicks out the punters' bills; it also, with a machine's indifference, rejects the cards of gamblers who have exceeded their credit."

On the floors above, 1,500 men and women sit at telephones or chalk odds on blackboards until, from some distant racecourse, the last sweating horses, before diminishing crowds, flash past the post. On the top floor with a view of the city and the House of Commons, whose Betting Act he so much deplored, William Hill has his office.

Hill is not a characteristic bookmaker. His suits and ties are smooth and dark. He breeds horses and cattle, he shoots, he is given to philosophising about the state of the nation, he is very, very rich. His attack on the Act is specifically an attack on Betting Shops, which the Act authorised, but his criticisms are of a general sort, on the growth of gambling, which the Act encouraged."

Hill told Morgan: "It's not sour grapes. Betting shops lay off their bets with me. But my objection to them is that they are having an adverse effect on the economy. Think of the man-hours that are wasted by people hanging around these shops. Whatever work these men should be doing, it is obvious that they are not doing it. I told the Government they would encourage more gambling and they have. Licences have been given to undesirables – gangsters and thugs, and to people who don't know the first thing about racing. We had spent a very long time making bookmaking respectable by clearing out the thugs and welshers, and now this Tory Government comes along and undoes all our good work."

"I don't know why people gamble," he went on, "perhaps their lives are dull. When I was a kid, you'd see lots of drunkenness in my home town, Birmingham. There were few cinemas and, of course, no telly, so all people had to do was to drink, and have a little bet. We don't see so much drunkenness these days, as young people have better things to do with their time, and few of them seem to bet. It's the adults who bet. I believe that with increased education there will be less gambling.

The bookmakers today are a lot of sheep. They follow their leaders. Once upon a time, a bookmaker had to use his initiative; now they are all like parrots imitating one another's odds. Most of them don't know the difference between a selling plate and a classic race."

Morgan went on to discuss with Hill the possibility of a betting tax, and Hill said that despite the endless discussion on the subject, politicians remained incredibly ill-informed on the subject of betting. Morgan continued:

"It was when I was talking about gambling taxes to Hill that he offered one of his more penetrating insights into the nature of the bookmaking business. Generally speaking the industry is a strange survival of 18th Century England. Along with his serious argument against the betting tax, on the grounds that the cost and difficulty of collection would make it uneconomic,

102

because the sums involved were less than anyone, including the Chancellor of the Exchequer, had been led to believe.

All cash businesses present a problem in that it is so easy to 'cook the books'. With a draper, it is easy to assess his takings, but you can't do that with a bookmaker, anymore than you can with barrow boys or publicans who all diddle the cash. If you see what I mean? You can imagine what a farce it would be. The bookmaker would keep two sets of books or, in other words, the Government would have driven betting and gambling underground."

Morgan concluded by saying: "Hill does not imply a profoundly anti-social quality in bookmakers; he has done as much as anyone to build a respectable structure into the profession. Even so, he presented a glimpse into a world in which tax evasion could be lightly borne as a moral burden, into the vertical seam of raffishness that reaches from the sophistication of the Stock Exchange and the metaphysical operation of the Merchant Banks, down to the half-dollar each-way double on the factory floor.

Betting is not simply a desire to get something for nothing. It takes in, too, the sense of isolation from society or responsibility that is part of the lure of gambling. Momentarily, the gambler is at his still, cool centre, a man alone, taking a chance. On this, no doubt, harmless 'play', or psychological need gangsters build little empires of their own. Ready cash, easily come by, throw long shadows in which seedy hoodlums and razor-boys flourish.

This is not to say that the many betting shops which have sprung up all over the country are run by crooks and hooligans. Their saddest feature is respectability and their discomfort. With a delicate hypocrisy, the Government has encouraged gambling by making the shops easily available, but salves its conscience by insisting they are graceless utilitarian places without coffee or soft drinks, and even without television to watch the horses." How very different in 1993!

Once he had risen to the top, William realised the value of shouting to the roof tops whenever a punter won a large sum of money from him. Although Littlewoods and Vernons soon got this down to a fine art, with reception committees at Grosvenor House or the Dorchester, and a well-known actress or TV personality handing over the enormous cheques to the dazed railway worker or Tyneside housewife, it was something of a novelty in the fifties and sixties for a bookmaker to advertise his losses.

Norman Pegg, *Gimcrack* of *The Daily Sketch*, wrote of William in the early sixties: "Very early in his career, William Hill started to advertise in a big way and it proved to be a short cut to the top. Today he is the undoubted King of the Ring. While his firm controls the ante-post market, Hill says that he loses over this form of betting. But it is difficult to believe that the millions who run the risk of not getting a run for their money when the horse is scratched should get the better of Mr. Hill, even though, on occasions, they obtain a better price than that at which the horse starts. Mr. Hill believes it pays to tell the world about the people who win from him, so he advertises, 'Mr. Stratford of Halifax won £16,000 for a 2s bet with William Hill on January 9' or 'Mr. Parker, at Windsor last week, won £24,744 from a £1 double at Tote odds.'"

16

A bookmaker must, of course, be prepared to lose every bet he lays, but he would have to be something more than human, if, on settling day, he did not kick himself from time to time for some of the losses he had incurred, while regarding others as being in a good cause.

An example was Airborne's Derby in 1946, for which he started at 50–1. When a great race is won by an outsider, it is usually safe to assume that the bookmakers have 'cleaned up' and although the Ring, as a whole, won handsomely on balance over Airborne's victory, a number of small bookmakers lost on the race, some of them quite heavily.

The war had been over for only a year, and large numbers of Airborne troops were still in the process of being demobilised, so it was natural that they should support the horse that bore the name of their units, rather than one of the favourites. Similarly, the friends and relatives of Airborne troops also supported Mr. Ferguson's horse.

So much 'small' money was there for the horse on the course that a fellow bookmaker asked William to lay him £10,000 to £150 as [£170,000 to £2,550] a hedging bet, and as he had laid Airborne to win only trifling sums, William agreed to do so. The small bets about Airborne took only about £1,000 out of William's book, and as they were to people who had backed the horse out of sentiment, William was delighted at their jubilation, and wished there had been more of them. However, that bet of £10,000 to £150 laid to a fellow bookmaker was very hard to bear.

Few backers boast about their losses, and even if they do, it is no advertisement for their bookmaker, but I would like to bet that at least one paratrooper, or member of an Airborne regiment, now elderly, and possibly bald and rather portly, is still boring the pants off his pals at the local, as he tells them for the umpteenth time how he backed Airborne at 66–1 with William Hill at the Derby, a minute before the off, all those years ago.

Bookmakers realise that in this imperfect world, everybody wants something for nothing, and when they get it they never stop talking about it. In 'the good old days,' before the Government started poking their noses into our expense accounts and entertainment allowances, bookmakers used to send us all sorts of goodies at Christmas, but now, alas, we are lucky if we get a calendar and a book of rules, which no one has yet been known to open.

The extent of a backer's credit was one of the problems which faced William Hill, as it does every bookmaker with a large clientele of punters. It has already been described how many bookmakers have been so greedy for custom that they have extended credit to men and women who would have no hesitation in defaulting if a settlement of their account would inconvenience them. William, being an excellent judge of character, and, in his heyday, having more accounts than his office could conveniently deal with, certainly did not come under this category, but there were occasions on which he and his other representatives on the rails had to make snap decisions as to when to say Yes and when to say No. The majority of backers have limited credit but it is seldom strictly adhered to, as a bookmaker cannot know exactly how much a client is winning or losing, since he or she received his or her last account. It is a headache which every rails bookmaker has suffered from when he sees a client approaching him whom he knows to be in the red.

Should he accept the bet and take the risk that the backer will sink further into the red? The decision must be made within a matter of seconds, and whatever that decision may be, he automatically offers a prayer that it is the right one.

The refusal of a bet must be made with the maximum tact, especially in the case of women backers. One might think that a backer's love life is no concern of his or her bookmaker, but, in the case of women, William believed that her love life was a very important factor indeed.

If a woman has a rich husband who worships the ground she walks on, a bookmaker would be very foolish to refuse her bet simply because she was losing rather more than her credit permitted. No bookmaker cares to be faced by an irate husband, especially if he is rich and declares: "How dare you insult my wife by refusing her bet." On the other hand, if the bookmaker learns that there are cracks showing in a marriage, he should remind the wife, with all the tact at his command, that she has over-run her credit, and if she suddenly wants to bet in bigger sums than she has ever wagered in the past, he should refuse her bets or suggest that she returns to her normal sized wagers.

Unmarried ladies were an even bigger problem to Hill, but, of course, I do not include those with large fortunes of their own. One of Hill's favourite sayings was: 'When love flies out of the window, the creditors knock on the door.' Peter Blackwell tells a story about the mistress of an enormously wealthy and very charming baronet.

The lady was beautiful, but in Peter's words, "Betted like a kicking horse." On one occasion, when she was deep in the red, she approached Peter and asked for a bet of £2,000. With all the charm (and he had plenty) at his command, Peter Blackwell declined her bet. He hated doing so, and wondered whether William would think he had done the right thing. Before he could explain to the guv'nor what had happened, the horse had run and lost, but William agreed that Peter had acted correctly. But they were both wrong, as a few weeks later, the baronet married her and, as far as I know, they both lived happily ever after.

William was called a lot of names, but I never heard anyone refer to him as a misogynist. However, he made no secret of the fact that, Dorothy Paget always excepted, he preferred doing business with men. He thought that the ideal woman punter should not be too young or too beautiful, unless, of course, she had a great deal of money of her own. William believed that when a woman has a number of creditors, the bookmaker is always the last to be paid.

Husbands and boyfriends have tried a number of ways to prevent their womenfolk betting above their means, but the most original and humane was conceived by an adoring husband whose wife was owing a very large sum indeed to William. He was a rich man and paid her losses in full but told William to continue to send her bill in every week, accompanied by dire threats of posting her at Tattersalls'. At the same time, he extracted a promise from William that he would not breathe a word to a soul about this honourable deception.

At the end of six months, the wife was at her wits' end and begged her husband to help. He relented and told her that the account had been settled several months before. She broke down and sobbed with gratitude, and I am happy to say she had learned her lesson. From that day she never had more than a tenner on a horse, and her account was always settled on the nail.

In the autumn of 1966, William laid the most sensational single losing bet of his entire career and, possibly, the most far reaching bet of all time. At a social gathering, largely comprised of racing men, William got into conversation with Vincent O'Brien who asked him, with a twinkle in his eye, if he had started to make a book on the 1968 Derby.

William roared with laughter as the runners for that race were still yearlings and had only just gone into training. O'Brien, however, expressed the wish to back three of his charges for the 1968 Derby if Hill would lay him 100–1 on each of them. William agreed, expecting that O'Brien would want no more than £50 on any horse which had only just gone into training and had never done a serious gallop for a race which would not be run for another twenty months. I do not know the names of two of the yearlings, nor do I know how much O'Brien invested on them, but I understand that the bets did not exceed £100.

The third colt was American-bred by Sir Gaylord out of Attica and O'Brien said he would like a 'monkey' (£500) each-way on him. Everyone, bar William, gave a gasp of astonishment when he accepted the bet without turning a hair, though he must have realised what he might be letting himself in for. The great William Hill, the most powerful bookmaker of all time, had offered a price about a horse, and to decline to accept a bet of £500 each way at those odds in the presence of this gathering of racing men was unthinkable. If, however, the son of Sir Gaylord and Attica showed any form as a two-year-old, William would be faced with a colossal liability.

William could have been forgiven if he had offered a prayer that the son of Sir Gaylord, subsequently named Sir Ivor, would not go to post for the 1968 Derby, but, if he did so, his prayer was not answered. Sir Ivor made his two-year-old debut at the Curragh in the Tyros Stakes over six furlongs on July 1, but, having started joint favourite, he could finish only sixth of the thirteen runners. Hill breathed a sigh of relief, but it was not long before it was brought home to him that his bet, laid the previous autumn, might prove the most costly of his career.

When making his debut, Sir Ivor had run very green, but in the Probationers Stakes over seven furlongs at the Curragh four weeks later, he revealed that he had not only learned a lot about racing, but was one hell of a horse in the making. Ridden by Liam Ward, he won a keenly contested race by a neck from Mistigo, the winner of the Tyros Stakes. Mistigo was giving Sir Ivor 5lb but all who watched that race would have bet their bottom dollar that Sir Ivor would beat Mistigo out of sight at level weights when next they met.

Sir Ivor's final outing as a two-year-old was in Ireland's most important race for juveniles, the National Stakes run over seven furlongs. Again ridden by Liam Ward, Sir Ivor 'murdered' his opponents, beating Candy Kane, who started favourite, by three lengths, with the third horse, Society, the mount of Lester Piggott, four lengths away in third. As Society had previously won the valuable Anglesey Stakes by two-and-a-half lengths, it did not require an astute student of form such as William Hill to realise that provided Sir Ivor survived the winter, his book on the Derby would read like a blood-curdling story devoid of a redeeming feature.

The bet had been struck by O'Brien on behalf of Sir Ivor's owner, Mr. Raymond Guest, but William's overtures, which would have proved irresistible to any man other than a million-aire, met with a courteous refusal. William offered Mr. Guest a very tempting hedging bet, but Mr. Guest realising that he had a bet in a million, replied, "Nothing doing."

Winter favourite for the Derby, Sir Ivor became an odds on chance following his victory in the Two Thousand Guineas. Lack of stamina in an odds-on Derby favourite had twice come to William's rescue. And he still hoped that Sir Ivor might not prove as effective over one-and-a-half miles as he had done over a mile. Lester Piggott had adopted somewhat exaggerated waiting tactics in the first classic, which suggested that he had some doubts concerning Sir Ivor's stamina. He had not given him his head until entering the final furlong, but when he did so his mount had swept by the second favourite Petingo to win by a length and a half. Twenty years earlier, William's lop-sided bet might have caused him considerable concern, but although a bookmaker never likes to be in the position William was in when he went to Epsom in June, 1968, he had taken quite a lot of money for some of the other horses.

The Derby is a race apart from all others and scores of people have a flutter on it who would not dream of betting on any other race. Odds of 6–4 on make no appeal to the once a year backer and, therefore, there is far more money on the outsiders than is normally the case. In the Derby, Lester Piggott adopted similar tactics to those which he had employed at Newmarket, and after Connaught had looked all over a winner, he brought Sir Ivor with a perfectly-timed run to win by the same margin as he had won the Two Thousand Guineas. William did not disclose whether he had lost over the Derby, but he was determined to capitalize over his 'disaster' as never before.

Sir Ivor had started at 6–4 on, and for the remainder of the season we were greeted with banners, headlines and reminders on TV that William Hill, the greatest bookmaker in the world, had laid a 100–1 to £500 each-way about an odds-on chance – something no bookmaker had ever done before. Once again, William Hill had proved that it's an ill wind. Truly, may it be said, you can't keep a good man down.

17

The credit goes to Bill Balshaw for giving William the final shove into the betting shop business, I doubt whether even he could have overcome William's obstinacy had not Jack Swift, a very intelligent and highly successful bookmaker decided to retire.

Unlike William, Swift had foreseen that it was only a matter of time, and possibly quite a short time, before half the volume of betting would be diverted from starting price offices to the betting shops, and immediately the shops were legalised, he set about securing suitable premises. William took over Swift's business and, therefore, became a betting shop proprietor. Even his obstinacy did not extend to closing down these already highly profitable establishments. Having become engaged in the betting shop business, his resistance was weakened when Balshaw issued his final ultimatum.

No man, having started with a few pounds from the till of his wife's hairdressing establishment and reached the pinnacle of his profession and became a millionaire in the space of twenty-five years, could help being an egotist, and William Hill was no exception. The modest man is prone to doubts and misgivings, but it never entered William's head that he would not be able to overcome difficulties which would have daunted any other man in his profession.

William was just as certain that he was the greatest bookmaker as Muhammad Ali is that he was the greatest boxer, although William was no exhibitionist, and was never heard to claim that he was without a rival in his chosen profession. The acceptance by a man such as William that he was number one bookmaker was not a token of conceit – he was merely being realistic.

He was, however, possibly with good reason, in constant fear that there were plotters on the prowl, and this suspicion increased after his retirement as a racecourse bookmaker. Standing on his box on the rails, he was a jovial warrior, and although he was accepting bets at the rate of twenty-five a minute, he had his finger on the pulse of the market, and his intuition was such that he could anticipate a market move for a particular horse. A man who acted as his clerk for some years told me that sometimes it seemed as if William was possessed of second sight. This man went on to say that though in the hectic twenty minutes or so prior to the start of the race, William might have laid hundreds of bets running into thousands of pounds, he knew how he stood to within a couple of hundred pounds.

Next to William, the most colourful figure on the rails was Willie Preston who died in 1986, betted for a number of years under the name of his father Alf Preston. William would indulge in caustic comment at the expense of a colleague who had turned down a bet; but he would never cross verbal words with a punter. Preston, however, carried on a constant flow of backchat with punters and bookmakers alike. Some of the sallies were highly entertaining, and although they were spontaneous, they must have interfered to some extent with the concentration essential to a bookmaker betting in the huge sums which William and Preston were betting for the first ten years after the war.

A passage of arms between William and Preston, sometimes friendly, and sometimes not so friendly, was a frequent occurrence, but proof of their mutual respect was forthcoming when, following William's retirement from the rails, Preston joined the firm of Hill's, and took his place on the number one pitch. "If you can't beat them, join them," someone quipped to Preston, but the king of the wisecracks did not think it funny.

If William overheard another bookmaker laying a point or two over the odds, he knew that it was for one of two reasons: either he was 'knocking it out', having backed it starting price, or he knew that it wasn't fancied, which, in bookmaking parlance, is known as 'dead meat'. With a nod of his head, and while still accepting bets, William would despatch one of his workmen to find out which of the two reasons had prompted this apparent generosity.

Every bookmaker has at some time or another knocked out a horse in the betting, and it is one of those practices which is quite permissible if you do it yourself, but entirely contrary to the ethics of bookmaking if performed by someone else. Like the rest of mankind, bookmakers can be hypocritical when their pockets are involved. I have heard the practice described as cheating, which it certainly is not, but it is desirable that it should not become an everyday occurrence. Fortunately, the leading bookmakers appreciate this, but a bookmaker, having paid for his pitch, is entitled to offer any price he likes about any of the runners. If he offers a shorter price than his colleagues, no punter, no matter how much of a mug he may be, will accept it, while if he offers over the odds, he is likely to be trampled under foot by an ugly rush of punters, all eager to take advantage of his generosity.

William had several 'workmen' on his payroll, whose job it was to ferret out information, which even his keen nose could not detect from his pitch on the rails. I once asked my brother what useful function a certain middle-aged man performed, whom I always saw lurking a few yards from the Hill representatives. He was obviously not a tic-tac man and did not appear to be a 'runner' or a 'minder'. "He knows all the villains", William explained.

There used to be several such men on all our racecourses, and so far as I know, they themselves were perfectly straight, though they may have been in close touch with members of the underworld.

In the fifties and sixties, if you 'lost' your binoculars or wallet on the racecourse and reported the loss to a bookmaker who happened to be a friend, it was more than likely he would say, "leave it to me, I'll sort it out." The odds were that in the next few days the article would be returned.

If William had a weakness, other than his obstinacy, which, I appreciate, is a contradiction in terms, it was that he was susceptible to flattery. Although he was incapable of bestowing praise, he liked to receive it, and it did not occur to him that his 'devoted admirer' might have an ulterior motive. No tycoon, unless he is a Howard Hughes, is entirely free from hangers-on, and when a man is fully occupied as William was, he does not bother to ask himself whether the friendly individual he met yesterday, who expressed such a sincere admiration for his talents, had an axe to grind.

Air Commodore Brooks relates how at the conclusion of one Royal Ascot meeting, when his box had been so full that no one could see anything of the racing, William made a vow that in future he would limit the number of his guests to half a dozen. However, on the day prior to the following year's Royal Ascot meeting, his telephone rang again and again a voice would say, "Bill, dear old boy, I haven't seen you for ages. Is there any chance of seeing you at Ascot?" And, of course, 'dear old Bill' would ask him to come along to his box and have a drink. And once again very little could be seen of the racing.

When a man was as successful and as self-sufficient as William, it is a relief to find that he had an Achilles' heel.

In addition to the parasites, William had a small number of life-long friends, who still talk of him with respect and affection. Throughout their business association, Lionel Barber was closer to him than anyone else at Hill House, but they were not, as many people believe, merely business associates.

Each realised how dependent he was on the other if the business was to function efficiently. But they also enjoyed each other's company out of business hours. No two men could have been more different. William the extrovert bookmaker, uneducated, but with a genius for figures who never stopped to count the cost. If he wanted anything from Whitsbury to a box of cigars, he bought it. His extravagance had appalled Lionel when the latter was called in to audit the accounts. But so impressed was he with William's ability that he left his own firm to join the Organisation. It was a lucky day for William when he did.

With the ice-cold brain of the Chartered Accountant, and the acknowledged number one authority on taxation, Barber was a man of few words, and was something of a cynic. When he told someone off, it was with a few carefully chosen words which cut like a knife. William's bluster left a few bruises which were soon forgotten, but a reproof from Barber took a long time to heal.

William and Barber remained the best of friends, both in and out of business hours for twenty-five years, but when the parting came the rift was so deep that they seldom spoke to one another again.

At the 1965 Annual Meeting of Holders' Ltd., Lionel Barber, the Chairman since the inception of the company twelve years earlier, disclosed a loss for the current trading year of £2½ million (and no declared dividend compared to that of 25 per cent for the previous year).

According to William, Lionel Barber, who had made his pile, and whose contract with the Organisation was due to expire in July, 1966, had been looking for an excuse to quit the book-making business for some time, and this adverse trading position provided him with the opportunity, as he put the blame entirely on William's shoulders.

Never a man to mince his words, William delivered a tirade against Barber, and denounced him before the Board of Directors at a meeting just before Christmas. On January 26, 1966, a headline appeared in *The Sporting Life*, 'Lionel Barber Resigns As Holders' Chief.' It happened to be premature, but a few weeks later Barber did, in fact, hand in his resignation, as did another director, Lt-Col R. S. Rogers.

At the time Hill was on his annual holiday in Jamaica, where he contracted an arthritic condition which necessitated his wearing a surgical collar. This was the first time he had been seriously ill since childhood, although he had continually fussed about his health, and those who knew him best had described him as a bit of a hypochondriac. In the early days of 1966, however, he was in continual pain, and his doctors feared that it might become a chronic condition. Fortunately, however, it yielded to treatment. So, too, did his ailing business, and the figures for the first three months of 1966 showed an increase in turnover of 15 per cent and the prospects of an overall profit of £1 million for the four months ending July 31.

Marriage to William Hill could not, by any stretch of the imagination, be described as unadulterated joy, but at no time in their forty-eight years of marriage was there a serious breach of their marital relationship. Ivy invariably accompanied William on his annual holiday to Jamaica, and he spent the weekends with her at Whitsbury, except when he was attending race meetings on the Continent.

In 1954, Ivy contracted a bug while on holiday with her husband in Las Palmas, which resulted in a chronic disease of the hip. For twenty years she was unable to walk without the aid of a stick, and suffered great pain, which she bore with great courage. Like all supremely successful egotists, William had his detractors, but I have yet to hear anyone say a disparaging word about Ivy.

Of his friends, the man for whom William had the greatest affection was Chesney Allen, a feeling which was reciprocated. Allen, partner of the late Bud Flanagan in so many unforgettable episodes of the Crazy Gang, described William to me as the greatest friend in a long lifetime.

In 1924, a year after their marriage, William and Ivy's only child was born – Kathleen Lavinia. She was nicknamed Bubbles, and her parents called her by that name throughout her life. They adored their lovely child, who was to grow up into a beautiful young woman. Educated at Roedean, she joined the Judge Advocate Generals' Branch of the U.S. Army in England in World War Two, and when serving in the U.S. forces, she met Matthew Leary, an American barrister doing his war-time service. They were married at the end of the war, and went to live at Burlington, in the State of Vermont. There were two children, a boy and a girl, but the marriage broke up in the early fifties and they were divorced. William went to the United States in an endeavour to secure custody of the children for his daughter, but after an acrimonious battle in the United States U.S. courts, he failed to do so.

Some years later, Bubbles met Edward St. George, brother of Charles St. George (who died in 1992), the highly successful racehorse owner. Like her first husband, Edward St. George was a barrister, but, having earned distinction at the criminal Bar, he was employed by the Crown Agents of the Colonies, and was stationed in Nassau. Two children were born of this marriage, both daughters.

Bubbles' tragic death from an overdose of sleeping tablets in 1961 has no part in this story. Her death was a shattering blow to her parents, and in their sorrow they turned to their closest friends, Mr. and Mrs. Chesney Allen, and with the Allens as their guests, they left for a quiet holiday at San Remo. Chesney Allen told me a long time ago:

"I first met William in the Old Vaudeville Club in Old Compton Street when he came to London in the late twenties, and from that day he and Ivy became our greatest friends. Ivy was an inspiration to him, and in those early days she worked in his office. The Old Vaudeville was a great rendezvous for variety artists, and was the headquarters of the Grand Order of Water Rats. We would meet and play snooker for a shilling a game, and though the stakes were so small, the rivalry was intense. All the Crazy Gang use to participate in these games, as did that great comedian Will Hay and jockey Charlie Smirke. Those were very happy days.

I introduced William to the Saints' and Sinners' Club, and he proved himself a marvellous member, and we blessed him for his generosity. For over thirty years, he donated £2,000 a year to the funds, and, in addition, he sponsored a number of races for our charity at Kempton Park. Those were the early days of sponsorship, before it became the big business which it is today. Although William invariably sought all the publicity he could get for his business, he was very reticent about his altruism. He would have preferred his donations to have been anonymous but I insisted that his name appear against his annual subscription. Even though we were nearest to him, however, I have no idea how much he gave away to those who had fallen on hard times. I was always mad keen on racing, and this was the bond between us. When I became an owner in a very small way, William took a keen interest in my horses, which I had in training with a little-known trainer called Bill Marshall, and I think I was in some way responsible for Bill Marshall getting the job as trainer at Whitsbury on the retirement of Sir Gordon Richards. We had been great friends since Bill Marshall was demobbed from the R.A.F., with a wonderful war record, and he had trained two horses of mine, Cuckoo Weir and Grecian Granite, who, between them, cost me just over £100, to win 22 races. Cuckoo Weir won three races in the space of ten days, and Grecian Granite won 17 races in all – from seven furlongs on the Flat to three miles over hurdles.

One day at Goodwood, William said to me, 'Your little trainer Marshall seems to do you pretty well, Ches, I should like to meet him.' We all had tea together and I left them chatting. The next thing I heard was that Bill Marshall had been appointed trainer to the powerful Whitsbury stable, where he has proved fantastically successful. Although most of the horses at Whitsbury cost many thousand of pounds, he still takes as much trouble over my humble animals which I bought for a few quid."

Chesney relates how on the day before they returned to England from San Remo, they decided to have tea at the casino, and William accompanied the Allens to the tables. Chesney went on to say that while he and his wife derived a lot of enjoyment from the mildest flutter, William stood open mouthed with astonishment that they should waste their time playing for peanuts. This anecdote portrays a side of William's character unknown to any but his intimate friends. He had a reputation for being a gambler, but in reality he was nothing of the sort. A gambler will bet on two flies crawling up the wall, for any sum you care to name, no matter how small or how big, but William betted only when he believed the odds were in his favour in what he considered worthwhile sums. It was inexplicable to him that eminently sensible people like the Chesney Allen's should play for a few lire with the odds stacked against them.

"How can you expect to win when this casino costs at least £100,000 a year to run, and also makes a huge profit?" William asked them. As they were his guests, they were too polite to answer: "Hill House, Whitsbury and Sezincote might lead one to believe that backing horses may not be all that profitable a pastime." No one, of course, realised that better than William, who did not purchase even one counter in the casino that after-noon. As usual, though, he was short of ready money, and borrowed £200 from the casino manager.

Chesney Allen is emphatic that he enjoyed the company of William more than that of any of his other friends – high praise from a man who spent his professional career in the company of some of the world's most entertaining characters. William was not a theatregoer in the accepted sense, but he loved the Crazy Gang. Chesney, however, thinks that *Monsewer* Eddie Grey be-came his favourite comedian following the death of Sid Field, another close friend.

Another close friend of William's was the boxer Jack Bloomfield, who was also a part-time bookmaker in the days when William was first making his way in the world. After his retirement from the ring, Bloomfield opened a club which was frequented by members of the stage and sporting world. It was destroyed by a bomb during the war, following which Bloomfield fell on hard times. William helped him financially and when he developed tuberculosis, paid all his expenses at a sanatorium in Switzerland. Jack made a partial recovery, but died in the early sixties.

Chesney Allen relates how William became 'an angel', i.e. he backed several plays, but even he could not tell me the reason for this uncharacteristic action, which conflicts with my assertion that he was not a gambler. Backing shows is well known to be the most speculative of investment, though if you are fortunate

enough to back a winner, the returns could be very remunera-
tive. Of the three shows William backed, two made a small profit
and one a small loss, so Chesney thinks he was a winner on
balance.

A possible reason for William's participation in the world of
the theatre is that he was interested in a member of the cast.
Chesney speaks nostalgically of the long weekends he and his
wife spent with William and Ivy at Whitsbury. William and
Chesney would go for long walks across the Downs. William,
apparently deep in thought, would not utter a word for sometimes an hour. Always a man who believed in minding his own
business, Chesney never intruded.

Although business always came before pleasure with William,
the women in his life were very important to him, and his leisure
hours required careful planning. Except on the racecourse where
he could win and lose thousands of pounds without turning a
hair, he was incapable of hiding his feelings, and wore his heart
on his sleeve for all to see.

On the two occasions when Quintin Gilbey accompanied
William to Paris, he was met at La Bourget by a brunette. Their
embrace was so prolonged that it caused some impatience to
those behind them who were queuing up with their parcels.
When one of the best known figures in the country is so demon-
strative, it inevitably gives rise to gossip, but this did not worry
William in the slightest. He had always been a glamorous figure
which pleased him and apart from the fact that he found the
company of women very congenial, his popularity with the
opposite sex was an asset to his business. Promiscuity, however,
had no attraction for him, and his extra marital relationships
were on a long term basis.

In 1969, William complained of severe chest pains, and his
doctor diagnosed angina. He was given pills to take when in
pain, he was warned to go carefully, and not to subject himself to
strain or tension. He followed these instructions, and the only
time he expressed concern was when he met his old friend, Jack
Cunnington, the Chantilly trainer, who told William that he also
had angina, and produced a pill several times larger than those
William had had prescribed. "Why the hell should Jack have
bigger pills than I've got?" he asked.

The pains became more frequent until the fateful day at

Newmarket on October 16, 1971. The previous evening he had sold thirteen yearlings from Whitsbury and Sezincote for a record sum, and he was having his breakfast in bed. Brooky and William's chauffeur, Mr. Smith, who also acted as his valet, were waiting downstairs to take him to the races. They found him unconscious on his bathroom floor in the Rutland Hotel, and he died shortly afterwards. Ivy lived on for about ten years.

Conclusion

The following is the address given by Phil Bull at the William Hill Memorial Service on November 12, 1971, and I am most grateful to Phil Bull for allowing me to include it in my story.

"We are here this morning to pay our last respects to a man who meant something to everyone of us, whom many of us held in great affection, and some of us loved.

It is my privilege to put my feelings and my tribute into words; for William Hill was my firm friend for over 30 years. Of his career as a bookmaker I shall say little. William began at the bottom of his profession, rapidly rose to the top and lifted the whole profession with him as he went.

He removed from bookmaking the check-suit and gold-watch chain image and gave it a new respectability and integrity. He became the greatest bookmaker of all time, both on the racecourse and off, with a centralised SP Organisation on a national scale such has not been seen before. It will not happen again. William's death was the end of an era. There will be none like him again.

William also made his mark upon the Turf itself. Cantelo, Nimbus and Grey Sovereign, were products of his studs. These, and the stallions he imported, Chanteur II, Ballymoss, Sica Boy, Celtic Ash, Taj Dewan and Gyr, will have a big influence upon the British thoroughbred for many years to come.

I wish to speak to you, however, not of William Hill the breeder, or the bookmaker, but of William Hill, the man. I will not pretend that he was a paragon. To those who worked with him he was a perfectionist who could be a demanding task master, sometimes too quick to criticise and blame, and all too slow to praise and compliment. He was flawed in other ways too. Which of us is not? But William was a man whose qualities of character far outweighed his failings and disabilities. Best of all, he had a real concern for justice and the welfare of people. Not theoretically, but practically.

121

During the war, his cashier at Hill House embezzled over £20,000 and was sent to prison for 12 months. Bill immediately provided the man's wife with a job and I was instructed to find a school for her two young sons. In the middle of the Flat season, we spent three days inspecting the school evacuated to Blanau Festiniog in North Wales. Bill then arranged for the education of the boys and also made a substantial donation to the school fund.

That experience gave me a regard for William Hill that nothing could every destroy. For a rich man to accept a financial responsibility is easy; for a man voluntarily to accept a moral responsibility that is not his, is another matter. But for a man to disregard the demands of his own pressing affairs and go to such trouble to help the dependants of someone who has just done him an injury, is an education in ethics.

This was but one of many such actions in the life of William Hill. He was a man scornful of snobbery, impatient of incompetence, rough and uncompromising in his judgments, and forthright in the expression of his views. He was a man of honour and integrity. He could be a very charming and considerate host. There will be few of us here who have not frequently enjoyed his hospitality. Few who have not received some kindness at his hand or been helped by him in one way or another.

The most important thing in life is not success in one's affairs but personal relationships. Friendship. We are lucky indeed if, in a lifetime, we make two or three real lasting friendships that are proof against all adversity and all vicissitudes. That was how it was between William and me. There were times when what he said or what he proposed to do, I could not countenance. No doubt he felt the same about me. But our respect for each other always bore the strain. And if my ship had run upon the rocks, he'd have been right there to throw the lifebelt to me.

To very many people, William's death will have brought a real sense of personal loss. That is its own tribute to him. My own personal loss is very real indeed. Most of the important events in the last 30 years of his life I shared. It seems that I stood beside him most of the way along the road – from the time I went with him to buy Whitsbury, until three weeks ago when they lowered his body into the grave in the churchyard there.

Watching there on that cold, sad day, I saw a little boy at the back of the classroom in a school in Birmingham, intent upon his painting, maybe dreaming that he'd be a famous painter one day. I saw the happy 12-year-old lad on a Warwickshire farm – the reluctant apprentice in a BSA tool room – the 18-year-old Royal Irish Constable, enlisted in his brother's name – and the newly-married 20-year-old, running a dance hall back in Birmingham. And then the young man in London, learning his trade on dog tracks, betting on the outside at Epsom, and making a name for himself at Northolt Park.

At last, I fancied I saw again the William Hill I lately knew, whose body they were lowering into its last resting place with all his other friends around. We are, all of us, the better for having known William Hill and the poorer for the loss of him. Let us then go on our various ways remembering him with affection."

THE VALUE OF MONEY

Editor's Note

Where possible in this book, as in the series *Great Racing Gambles & Frauds*, I have inserted after the actual figures concerned, a possible modern day equivalent following the lead set by my friend, Paul Mathieu in his brilliant book *"The Druids Lodge Confederacy"*. The Retail Price Index was only started in 1914. Since 1914 the Government, via it's Central Statistical Office, has produced an index of retail prices which makes comparisons readily available. I must express my deep gratitude to the Press Officer and his colleagues of the Central Statistical Office for their help in compiling these books. They have spent many hours on the telephone explaining their weird and wonderful figures.

However, prior to 1914, there are many different expert opinions on the value of money as Paul Mathieu said to me in a letter:

"Divide 433.95 [sic] by the Index number and – Hey Presto! – you have an equivalent for the £1 of today.
This of course fails to take into the account the fact that today's RPI is based on the price changes of commodities – baked beans, detergents, mortgages, video recorders – that were hardly in plentiful supply in 1791, or indeed 1891. But it's the only measurement available."

I have discussed the value of the pound from the 1790s to 1900 with various experts at Universities and the Librarians of such distinguished journals as the *Financial Times* and the *Economist*. Some maintain that there was little falling of the value of money in the 19th Century while others argue it was fairly dramatic. I personally believe that there was a substantial decrease in the purchasing power of money in the first 110 years covered by this book and I have used the figures set out below in my computations.

The figures prior to 1900 are highly questionable and different academics will produce radically different figures but I hope they will give some idea to the reader of the sums involved.

"1991/1994 Value of Pound in"

1780 – 1799 –	£375
1800 – 1819 –	£350
1820 – 1839 –	£230
1840 – 1859 –	£170
1860 – 1879 –	£120
1800 – 1899 –	£80
1900 – 1919 –	£44
1920 – 1939 –	£32
1940's	– £17
1950's	– £13
1960's	– £8
1970's	– £5

One academic suggested that the value of today's pound in 1820 would have been £2,000 and due to deflation £3,500 in 1840 and £4,000 in 1850. So the figures above are very much E & OE.

A curate in one of Charles Dickens' books in 1840 says "I have made my fortune, I have secured a living of £35 a year". What is a living for a Man of the Cloth? Certainly he wasn't going to be paid the equivalent of £125,000 a year which a multiplier of 3,500 would indicate, but he would have been paid more than £6,000 which my multiplier of 170 would indicate.

I am afraid it is nearly an insoluble conundrum.

R.C.

Captions for Photographs

129   William with five of his brothers and sisters. He is the smaller boy without a cap to the right rear.

130   Be Careful winning the 1958 Gimcrack Stakes at York.

131   William, bowler hatted, at Longchamp after Ballymoss' win in the 1958 Prix de l'Arc de Triomphe.

132   Cantelo, E Hide up.

133   William in the winners enclosure after Cantelo's victory in the 1959 St. Leger. Phil Bull is partially obscured by William's hat.

134   Gyr at stud, 1970.

135   Ballymoss at stud, 1973.

136   William with 'Peter' Parsons.

129

131

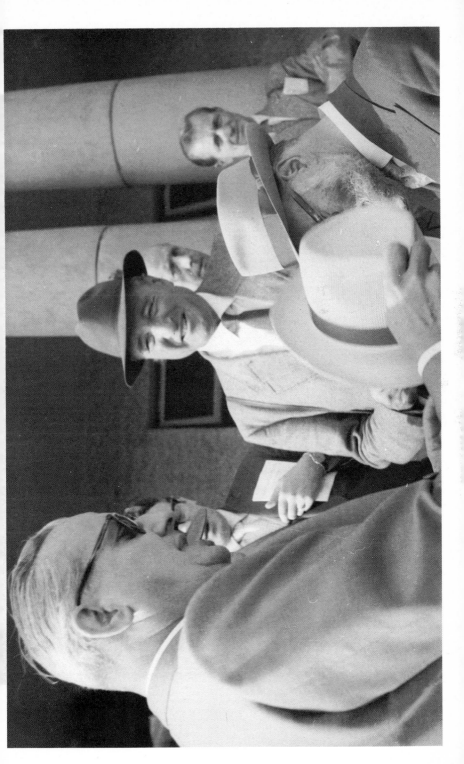

134